Digging a Well

www.diggingawell.blogspot.com

Digging A Well

Copyright © 2012 by Sherry S. Long
All rights reserved. No part of this book may be reproduced or transmitted in any form or by any means, electronic or mechanical, including photocopying, recording or by any information storage and retrieval system, without permission in writing from the copyright owner. This book was printed in the United States of America

This book was printed in the United States of America

Because of the dynamic nature of the internet, any web addresses or links contained in this book may have changed since publication and may no longer be valid.

All Scripture quotations,
Unless otherwise indicated,
are taken from the
Holy Bible (King James Version)
1769 authorized version.

CONTENTS

Acknowledgement
Foreword
Dedication

Chapter One	Heritage	1
Chapter Two	Painting a Book	7
Chapter Three	Abraham's Well	19
Chapter Four	Bitter Water of Marah	29
Chapter Five	Well of Salvation	41
Chapter Six	What Stops your Well	57
Chapter Seven	No Way	69
Chapter Eight	River of Life	75
Chapter Nine	Leave my Children Alone	89
Chapter Ten	Greatest Lover of all Times	97
Chapter Eleven	Getting Ready for the Trip	107
Conclusion	Which Well Will You Dig?	117

A GOOD HERITAGE IS LIKE A BANK
IN THE MIDDLE OF THE DESERT,
DRAWING A CONSTANT SUPPLY OF WATER
EVEN DURING THE DRIEST TIMES.

ACKNOWLEDGEMENTS

To my husband Steve, who always preaches the word of God each time he delivers a message. You helped me with proofing and inspired me to write the song, "Empty I Come to You." You have challenged me to stretch in areas I didn't think were possible.

To my children who are so patient with me and love me no matter what. You continue to teach me lessons in life and continue to bless me abundantly when I see how wonderful you each have become.

Joshua Long is a staff pastor at a church in the Dallas area. Josh is married to Kristy and together they have given us two beautiful grandchildren, Emma and Noah.

Josh, you inspire and give me words of wisdom so many times. Most of the time you don't realize it but the Lord has used you to show me what true compassion is and much more.

Lisa, our second child, lives in the Dallas area and works at Citibank. She has helped me with many brochures for ladies' events, and has a voice that is angelic. She has supported me by using her musical talents and writing abilities.

Lisa began a summer youth program called Indignus (meaning unworthy.) We are all unworthy but the Lord called us out and is willing to use us. This was one event that was at the forefront of change for Northside Baptist Church. God used this event along with a couple other events to change the flow of our well.

Lisa, your knowledge was valuable to me in so many ways.

Your strength to endure through continuing medical hardships is unsurpassed.

Matthew, our youngest son, also living in the Dallas area.. He has his own band and works at a coffee shop. Matt also makes me a cup of coffee with a heart floating on top. His artistic ability comes out in every area of his life.

Matt, you melt my heart with the way you say, "I love you, Momma."

My sisters have spent many hours listening to my questions and giving wonderful words of advice. I couldn't have completed this book without the help of

Kay Rowe and Balinda Zimmerman. My sister, Kathy Mitchell, stood beside me for over a year while I was at the side of my own Well of Despair. She gave me a place to heal and stood beside me in so many ways.

Thank you Balinda, Kathy and Kay for standing with me and being the greatest sisters a girl could ever have. Balinda you went above and beyond to make sure this was a great book, hanging with me for the last few weeks through all the changes and submitting for print.

A special thanks to Bobbie Dale Cotton and Joyce Cotton Crawford for your love and patience and for the many hours of corrections you willingly gave.

Thanks to Carol Garborg, Amy Hailey and Mary Boydston and Fay Palmer for your constant prayer support, and encouragement. Carol, thanks for taking the time to review this book and for all of your help,

Most of all, thanks to my wonderful Savior and Lord for walking with me, leading me and guiding me through the process of my life

FOREWORD

Water is something we can't do without, yet seldom is it thought about until we're dealing with a drought. It's in those dry seasons that the value of water is truly realized. Sherry Long wears many hats; however, the one that best fits her is the one of a pastor's wife. Her compassion for women's issues drives her passion to help them drink from the Well of Living Water. Her aspiration is to lead women to the well that never runs dry.

I've had the pleasure of being one of the original members of "Digging a Well Ministries" and have seen God use Sherry to help restore broken lives. Just as everybody requires water to survive, every soul requires the "Living Water" flowing from Christ to thrive. In this book, Sherry masterfully shows us that we're naturally drawn to wells to quench our thirst.

The choice is ours whether to drink from wells of bitterness, destruction or salvation. We often don't realize how the wells we dig or drink from will affect the rest of our lives and others who drink after us.

Sherry points out, "Abraham, Isaac, Jacob and many other men dug wells. As they traveled across the land, they would dwell in one location awhile and dig a well for their families to live and their stock to drink from. Later on, Jesus himself was sitting at a well that Jacob dug hundreds of years before. When Jacob was traveling thru the land, do you think he ever thought that the Messiah himself would someday drink from his well? Yet there he was. He even offered the Samaritan woman a drink. He asked her to drink the Living Water that only he could give."

As we do this thing called life, we often become encumbered by our own struggles and forget someone else may come our way in need. By doing this, we risk missing out on the greatest blessings. If Jacob had dug a well of unsuitable or bitter water, the Savior might not have used it to bring salvation to the Samaritan woman and thus, many others.

Sherry brings this to light by using colorful illustrations in her career such as when she saved the life of a baby from being taken. She lovingly showed the young woman the Father's grace and mercy through a mother's eyes and helped her to a Well of Salvation.

Sherry also interestingly uses geological information to give us a unique perspective of spiritual truths. As she names and correlates vital parts of a well to the church body, it's clear that Jesus is our pipe and pressure vessel. It's impossible for a well to function correctly without them. They are "designed and constructed in accordance with a health and safety standard incorporated into these regulations. Jesus Christ was made to be our pressure vessel. He was tried and tested in every possible way, yet he never gave in to the temptation. Thus, Jesus would meet up to the highest standard possible."

The insights that Sherry shares in this book are both unique and timely as we go through seasons of droughts. It's imperative to help people identify faulty thinking and aid their search for another direction. Sherry not only changes streams of faulty thinking, she also directs us to a Well of Living Water, which will never run dry.

Happy Digging, Jonean Walton, M.A.

DEDICATION

On Sunday morning in April of 2010, Jonean asked me once again, "Sherry, When are you going to write a book?" In such a sarcastic way I turned to her and said, "OK Jonean, it's like this – If – get that with a capital, IF God sends me to the mountains, I will write!"

Little did I know that God had already lined out the trip by paving a way through our youth group.

The youth from Northside Baptist Church had just planned to go to the Guadalupe Mountains on Saturday for a hiking trip of which I was unaware when I had made the statement. During the announcements that Sunday, James Cotton said the youth would be taking a trip. It never crossed my mind what God was doing. Steve and I had never gone on any of the youth trips thus far at Northside so I assumed this one would be the same.

On Tuesday my husband was driving down the road and said, "I'm going to the mountains Saturday, want to go?"

I instantly said, "What!"

He once again said, "I'm going with the youth Saturday to the mountains, do you want to come with us?

I took a very deep breath and looked at him as if to say, "I really can't believe you just asked me if I would like to go to the mountains."

At this point, I was in total shock and he didn't really understand why.

I finally stated, "Yes! I really don't want to go but I think that I'm supposed to go to the mountains."

Arriving back home, a call was placed to Jonean, letting her know of our planned trip to the mountains. At this point Jonean began to scream,

"NO WAY! NO WAY!
HIP, HIP, HURRAY!"

A few days later there was a pulse pen on my kitchen table. Jonean had felt the Lord lead her to purchase this item for me. This pen records while I take notes during interviews. This one item has been more help to me than anyone could ever imagine.

I now had to keep my promise to Jonean and the Lord to write this book.

Jonean has now been labeled, "My Feet." This is a title that we both treasure, for you see, Jonean is in a wheelchair. This chair does not confine her from using her spiritual feet to further the gospel of Jesus Christ. Jonean is also a writer and in the process of publishing a book.

Jonean Walton lives on a ranch in Kermit, Texas. Never giving up on me, she would ask every Sunday, "When are you going to write a book"?

So Jonean, here goes!

*Allowing the perfect peace of Christ
To have control to the point where,
His Spirit settles over your soul.
Captivating your inner being to be still
And know that He is God.*

The Path is long and lonely,
But it will strengthen up your life
If in those dark and dreary times
For peace, you turn to Christ.

DIGGING A WELL — HERITAGE

CHAPTER ONE

HERITAGE

What is your water source? Where do you get the ideas and motivations that run through your veins? Why do you think the way you do and say the things you say?

Our heritage plays a major role in our lives. It helps us make decisions, think through things, or relate to people the way we do. My heritage is very rich! My grandmother, Mamie Creekmore, whom we affectionately called "Granny," was an extremely strong willed person. Early in her life she determined that she would live her life by the following verse.

"...that for me and my house,
we will serve the Lord".
Joshua 24:15

DIGGING A WELL — HERITAGE

Her life has inspired many of her children, grandchildren and now great-grandchildren to be servants of Christ.

Granny has written some wonderful Christian songs, which can be found in her book, "Words from Granny." She taught Sunday school and worked at the Baptist Associational Office in Tennessee. She placed a very sweet taste of what true Christianity is onto the palates of her children, grandchildren and great-grandchildren.

When Granny passed away in 2009, at the age of 91, this was the spiritual legacy that she had left behind. Preachers in her family are two sons, one son-in-law, four grandsons, one grandson-in-law, and three great grandsons. She also has one granddaughter who is a pastor's wife. Her granddaughter has worked at the Baptist Associational Office with Bro. Darold Baldwin in Snyder, Texas and with Jeff Ford at the Baptist Student Center in Wichita Falls. She has written 5 songs and now is authoring this book. Our family's aquifer is rich with deacons, deacon's wives, nurses, servicemen, community leaders, vocalists, writers, and the list goes on.

> *"Whosoever drinks the water*
> *I give will never thirst.*
> *But the water that*
> *I give him shall be in him*
> *a well of water springing*
> *up into everlasting life."*
> *John 4:14*

Granny was the main channel of the living water for our family. She is part of our aquifer. According to dictionary.com an aquifer is: any geological formation containing or conducting ground water, especially one that supplies the water for wells, springs, etc.

The process of removing water from an aquifer requires pressure. When you are placed under pressure and squeezed, what begins to flow from your life? Do you flow with words of wisdom or words of vulgarity? Do you show courage and strength during the greatest trials in your life or do you throw your hands up in the air and quit?

My grandmother, being the aquifer for the Creekmore family, set such a godly example for each of us. When she was pressed or squeezed, we never saw her turn to abuse. The thing she showed us flowing from her life was Jesus Christ, the Living Water. This was seen on a daily basis through songs she would write, people she would love, and her faith in the Almighty God.

When a person has a solid aquifer and the foundation is Jesus Christ, others will notice. When that foundation has been one of abuse, drugs and alcohol, it becomes that person's tendency to have a gusher of foul language, abuse or murder erupting from the aquifer. …..

> *...for out of the*
> *abundance of the heart*
> *the mouth speaketh.*
> *Matthew 12:34*

If our lives are filled with the Holy Spirit, there will be no room for any other substance. When a cup is filled to the brim with water, you can't pour oil into the cup. The oil will just slide off the water onto the table. This is true with the Living Water. If a life is *filled* with the Holy Spirit, there isn't room for the things that Satan tries to pour into our daily lives.

DIGGING A WELL — HERITAGE

> *"And be not drunk with wine,*
> *wherein is excess; but be*
> *filled with the Spirit;"*
> *Ephesians 5:18*

My dear, sweet grandmother taught me many lessons about laying a solid foundation. Remembering how she lived her life has provided one of the greatest resources for writing this book.

My grandfather taught me things about his Indian heritage that made me stop and ponder. He would never talk about his culture but it was woven very deeply into his veins. One couldn't help but notice the difference in personality and ways of life.

Closing my eyes, I remember back as a very small child watching my grandfather, William Fines Creekmore. He would take a stick that was sort of shaped like a wishbone and walk across a patch of land searching for water. If the stick began to bend toward the ground, he would stop and see if it continued to have a downward pull.

As I think back on this I am shown a very valuable lesson. Many people think that this example signifies witchcraft. It was something passed down in the Cherokee tribe for many generations in our family.

There still is a biblical lesson to be learned in this process. When he would come to a place where there was water, the stick would start to pull toward the earth.

> *So is every person that is born.*
> *We all have a natural pull to the*
> *Living Water, "Jesus Christ".*

DIGGING A WELL — HERITAGE

We are born with the desire to learn who created us. Why are we here on this earth? Who makes everything hold together? We all understand that somehow somewhere, there had to be someone greater than ourselves.

We may not have the knowledge to grasp who God is, but we all know there had to be someone who put all the majesty and glory of the creation together.

The following poem was written as I began to realize that my grandparents would soon be passing from this life. I began to think about the importance of not just living from day to day for myself. I have seen the value of passing on from generation to generation the rich heritage that I was given.

PASSING THE BATON

When passing the baton, the baton in this life
Did I hold it too loose? Did I hold it too tight?
Did I show you just how, to give it to others?
To pass it real smoothly,
So they can discover.

Did I teach you to run with joy in your heart?
To cherish his word….to never depart?
Did you learn how to smile,
Through the deep, dark struggles,
Of running the race not for yourself
But for others?

The others that watch but don't understand,
Who need to take Jesus as Savior and friend.

HERITAGE

They see you struggle, the hurt and the pain.
They see you turn to Jesus,
And worship His Name.

This is the baton I want to pass on.
So that others see Jesus
And they will grow strong.
They'll take the baton and give it to others
And pass it along from sister to brother.
Passing, still passing, as the years go on,
Not ever forgetting the race that Christ has run.
So set before you the wonderful prize
The mark, the high calling,
Of the Lord Jesus Christ.

We will stand before Christ
Some wonderful day,
Saying, "Satan was defeated
When you rose from the grave."
Living victorious so others could see.
I've brought my friends and family
To heaven with me.

And now we will bow and fall on our knees,
Casting our prize and crowns at your feet.
The one that deserves
All praise that is due,
Heaven and Earth stops,
JUST TO WORSHIP YOU.

CHAPTER TWO

PAINTING A BOOK

The paper, my canvas;
The pencil, my brush.

If, when I write, you can't envision my words with color, then I've not accomplished writing this book in its entirety. When you paint a picture with words, you should be able to envision the rich colors in your mind. You should be able to feel yourself as if you were right there when it happened. You should be able to almost taste the flavor.

Right now, stop reading and envision yourself as the one bowing in the presence of the most Holy God and giving him all your worship and all of your praise.

As we were traveling to the luscious, green state of

DIGGING A WELL   PAINTING A BOOK

Arkansas for a mission trip, we stopped at our son's house in Garland, Texas. Our granddaughter is the joy and the delight of our lives. She truly is grand in every way.

She is learning to talk and learns new words every single day. I love more than anything in life to watch her – watch her struggle to form the new words on her tongue, then give me the most adorable look and start giggling.

Our Emma seems to be the happiest baby on earth, especially if she can tug at her Papa or MeeMee's heart to get one of us to take her outside. She is like Gumby at this point in her life. Whatever direction someone is going, that is where Emma goes.

Her beautiful hazel eyes are glued intently to every movement. If her Papa walks backward, Emma walks backwards. If Papa bends down to pick up something, Emma bends down to pick up something.

Emma has her own stove and refrigerator in the dining room. You can tell she has watched her Mommy and Daddy intently as they were cooking meals. She will be playing and then look at her MeeMee and say, "Cook!" She stops what she is doing and runs to her little kitchen. She places her apron over her head and asks her Mommy to tie it in the back. She gets her pan and spoon and away she goes.

As I watched her, I began to see that our precious little Emma is like play dough. Every person that touches her life during the next few years will actually be shaping and forming her into the young lady she will become one day. There will be people that have red play dough and as they touch our little Emma's life some of the red is mixed in. Her life will be filled with excitement and laughter. There will be people that form the color blue. They will be an example of peace and contentment. There will be so many people forming her life, that at times it is actually overwhelming, scary, and yes, also exciting. It is very important that during those years we do as the Bible says.

> *Train up a child*
> *in the way he should go,*
> *and when he is old,*
> *he will not depart from it.*
> *Proverbs 22:6*

Christians are really condemned by the media for brainwashing children. I watch as so many lives are shaped and formed by television, computer games, and even by liberals who don't believe in brainwashing. Or is it just that they don't believe in shaping and forming little minds to believe in Christ, to love the Lord their God with all their hearts, with all their souls and all their lives?

Our school books teach our children that the earth is billions of years old and mankind started out as monkeys and we just move forward all the time to being better. When I look at mankind, I see we are increasing in knowledge but as for becoming better, that is still in question. It seems the more knowledge we acquire, the less we feel we need the wisdom of the Lord. This teaching is contrary to the scripture. They seem to feel it's alright to teach them a theory for twelve to fourteen years that hasn't been proven – just a theory.

Every culture believes in a Higher Power. Even primitive people, who haven't been given the gospel of Christ, seem to know there is someone greater than themselves. They understand that they were created and placed there by someone. For some reason, many people just don't want to admit that the Higher Power is Jesus Christ.

We began to teach our children at a very early age that;

DIGGING A WELL
PAINTING A BOOK

"In him we live, and move, and have our being."
Acts 17:28.

God is the one that took a paintbrush and dipped it into the most awesome colors ever. As he dipped the brush into the blue, he painted the sky. He then dipped the brush into white and painted the sun, moon and stars. With the green, he painted the trees and grass. Then he began to dip the brush into all the other colors. He mixed colors he designed and created until his heart was content.

He continued on and on as he created the peacock, deer, rabbit, bear, sheep, and the birds. When he stopped, he still felt something was missing.

Thus far, it was just a painting on a canvas. There was nothing to really pour his soul into. If you have given birth to or fathered a child, you know the feeling before and after that moment. Many times we are satisfied, but not really content.

"Ah! Let's see. I wonder what it would be like to paint someone just like myself."

Someone to walk with!
Someone to talk with!
To laugh with! To sing with!
Ah! But most of all,
Someone to love!

As he painted onto the canvas a man, he realized there was something still missing. "Ah, I need to breathe within him my air, my breath."

The first case of CPR ever performed was on a canvas in

| DIGGING A WELL | PAINTING A BOOK |

Genesis. The Lord God Almighty performed it. He is loving, holy, just, and perfect in every way, yet he bent down and placed his mouth upon the mouth of mankind. Did he stop there? No! He breathed into him the breath of life.

Close your eyes and imagine just what it would feel like to be the first man. You are lying there on the ground one moment as dust from the earth. The next moment you open your eyes and God himself has given you life.

Real life!
Abundant life!
Eternal Life!

You, my child, are God breathed! You open your eyes for the first time. You are stunned at the beauty of everything you see. You are surrounded by the richest odors of nature. Deep breaths, more deep breaths, and your lungs fill with oxygen. The colors are so rich you can smell them. It is the fragrance of beauty that you are surrounded by. The sounds of the leaves rustling in the wind captivate your attention. What has just taken place? Where am I? How can this be happening? This is beauty beyond what anyone can fathom.

Never touched by sin,
death, and evil,
It was radiant, vibrant, and glorious!

You would be able to run through the fields with no need for shoes, no need for clothing, no need for anything. You would be perfect in every way. There would never be the thought of a bad desire, no cravings for evil – no cravings for anything except for the presence of God. Every breath would be that of purity. The air, pure and clean, would be like none we've ever experienced and the earth, created in perfection.

Most of all,
Your spirit and your soul
would be pure.

Do you ever long for that life? Do you ever wish you could just rewind the clock or jump into a time machine and change the past? Are there times you desire to get away from everything and just sit in his presence? Do you long to soak in his abundant beauty and majesty?

Oh my! Is that the washing machine that just finished and needing the clothes moved to the dryer? Not again! One of the children has fallen and skinned his knee. The phone is ringing for the fourth time, "I guess I had better answer it." You look around and feel compelled to go back into your sanctuary to bask in the presence of the Almighty God, to be swept away into what you can only imagine heaven must be like.

We can only imagine how the Garden of Eden must have looked after the Lord touched his brush upon it. We stand back and try to envision the beauty, but we just can't quite get there because the canvas has been tainted with darkness. This darkness entered onto the canvas at the time that Eve listened to the voice of the serpent. What would you have done had you been Eve?

Each of us is given a canvas of our own to paint. I so enjoy painting upon my canvas in the springtime. My children used to laugh at me every spring as I would shop for flowers and potting soil and begin to create in my mind what I wanted our yard to look like. After a few weeks of ridding the flower beds

DIGGING A WELL / PAINTING A BOOK

of all the weeds that had grown over the months, I would then begin planting the new flowers. Steve would start pruning any bushes that needed pruning. I would call the boys out to mow the yard. After all this had been completed, I would gather all the kids into the car and we would go for a ride. We would drive by our own house slowly and I would tell the kids to look closely.

I would say out loud, "Ah now just look at that yard, isn't that a pretty yard?" Then I'd say, "Don't you think the family that lives in that house really takes good care of their yard?"

This is exactly what the Lord did. He created the heavens and the earth on the first day. Then he said,

"This is good."

In other words, he looked at his own painting and was satisfied, but only satisfied. After he had created each thing, he would step back and ponder what he wanted to add next. Each time he must have thought to himself, "There is still something missing."

I must admit something. I'm not much into talking during a movie but I come alive when a commercial comes on. Steve laughs at me because we will sit there for fifteen minutes and I will not comment once on the movie but as soon as the commercial comes on, things change. I love the beauty and excitement that they show during commercials.

The commercial by Lowes Home Improvement shows a lady getting ready for springtime. She walks into her garage and picks up a roll of carpet, walks out to her front lawn and unrolls it. It is filled with lusciously green grass. The flowers are blooming in every color. There are butterflies fluttering around in excitement at the fragrance. Ah, perfect beauty!

The beauty is so perfect that I could never achieve it. I know that I will never even come close. But each time I see the

DIGGING A WELL — PAINTING A BOOK

commercial I am overwhelmed at how beautiful the yard becomes in just a matter of minutes. I can only imagine the beauty of what the earth looked like when God painted his picture on the canvas of this world.

Finally on the sixth day, he created mankind (man and woman) and breathed into them the breath of life. He stepped back to look at his canvas and said, "AH! THAT IS VERY GOOD."

The Lord God Almighty was not just satisfied he was very satisfied. Do you feel when he looks upon you that he says, _____, I am very satisfied?"
(Fill in your name here)

Just as our heavenly Father made the choice of what colors to paint our world, each parent that has given life to his or her child also has that choice. You have the option of painting your child's small mind with one or two colors or doing as your heavenly Father did. He dipped the brush in every color and painted our world a vibrant array of colors.

I am so blessed that Josh and Kristy are painting little Emma's world bright and beautiful. They are doing exactly as the scripture says.

> *And thou shalt teach them diligently unto*
> *thy children and talk of them when*
> *thou sittest in thine house, and when*
> *thou walkest by the way*
> *and when thou liest down*
> *and when thou raiseth up.*
> *And thou shalt bind them for a sign*
> *upon thine hand,*

> *and they shall be as frontlets*
> *between thine eyes.*
> *And thou shalt write them upon*
> *the post of thy house,*
> *and on thy gates.*
> *Deuteronomy 6:7-9*

This sounds like no matter what we are doing, we need to have the Lord God visible to us and to our children. I'm blessed to hear that Josh & Kristy tell Emma what God created for her to enjoy. As they walk down the hillside, they tell her that the Lord painted the trees and grass green so she can enjoy them. When Josh takes Emma in the canoe, he points out to her that God gave them the blue sky, the sun, the moon and the stars.

Emma just now turned two years old. She constantly is pointing and saying, "grass, trees, birds, kitty, doggy, bug, Lisa, Mommy, Daddy, nose, eyes, Matt, Nanna, and PawPaw." Then all of a sudden her eyes brighten up and she says "'side, swing" and she will run to the back door which means she wants you to take her outside to swing. After a few minutes of swinging she will say, "It's fun!" These are her carefree moments and nothing else seems to matter. She could swing all day long if you let her.

Her little world is being shaped and molded. She is forming fond memories at this point in her life that will actually shape her into a young lady one day. She is learning right from wrong. She is learning when to talk and when to be silent. She is truly like a piece of play dough, but the older she becomes the harder it will become to shape her life.

Does this mean that we should just drill all of these

concepts into our children's lives at once? No. I have seen many parents that actually did this to their children and usually the outcome wasn't very good. The scripture says that we should make it a part of our everyday life.

> *Walk with the Lord,*
> *talk to the Lord,*
> *Sing to the Lord,*
> *pray to the Lord,*
> *and truly love the*
> *Lord your God*
> *with all your heart,*
> *with all your soul,*
> *and with all your might.*
> *Taste and see that*
> *the LORD is good.*

It is important for us to place the word of God on the palate of their mouth and leave the taste of something very sweet so they will have a desire for more.

Our Father God set the perfect pattern for us. He painted a picture of how we are to form our children, our grandchildren and yes, even our great-grand children's lives. It is quite a challenge but it is also quite rewarding.

Steve and I have slowly added the strokes of color, a little red, blue, purple, and a dab of pink, green, brown and yellow. Now our children are grown and on their own, I can step back as a mother, look at my precious children and say, "This is very good". Not to just say, "This is good" but to say, "This is very good."

Are they perfect? By no means! Is mankind perfect? By no

means! But we are created in the Father's image and that is very good.

Each one of us will be painting pictures in the lives of our posterity. We get the opportunity to have each of these people stop and sit with us, study with us, and drink with us. My challenge to each of you is to look at the different wells in the scripture, seek the Lord's face, pray and ask him which well he would have you to be. When others drink from your well, they will not just be changed but they will be forever changed.

If you are a Christian, then I challenge you to be sure that people you are surrounded with have the opportunity to drink from the Well of Salvation. In doing so, they will experience the living water. We live in a world that is thirsty and in need of that thirst being quenched.

Many times, we try to fill our thirst with relationships, clothes, shoes, money, houses or new furniture. Then, after we have attained them, we are still thirsty. We run to something else to quench our thirst. We go out and buy new cars, take vacations to wonderful places, and do things we have never done before. Are those things wrong? No, not at all! Yet in the stillness we realize our thirst is still not quenched.

Jesus Christ is the Living Water and only he can satisfy our souls.

As the hart panteth
after the water brooks,
so panteth my soul after thee,
O God.
Psalms 42:1

We see in the scripture that wells were not just holes in the ground from which to draw water, and not just a spot in the middle of the city where the townspeople met to fill their pots. These wells are actually a picture of what the Lord wants in our lives. As we travel though each chapter, ask yourself this question.

"Which well do I choose to represent to my family and friends?"

CHAPTER THREE

ABRAHAM'S WELL

*And he looked, and saw
a well in the field;
and behold, there were three flocks
of sheep lying by it; for out of
that well they watered the flocks.
A large stone was on the well's mouth.
Now all the flocks would be gathered there;
and they would roll the stone from the
well's mouth, water the sheep, and put
the stone back in its place
on the well's mouth.
Genesis 29:2-3*

DIGGING A WELL — ABRAHAM'S WELL

Can you just imagine back in time? "Abraham! Abraham! The baby's coming." " Hurry, gather some hot water!" Can you just imagine the dilemma that the women in the Bible days faced? Even if Sarah had a pot to put the water into, you can only imagine how unclean it must have been. The tent in which she lived had no double pane windows, no screens or no caulking to keep the wind and rain out. Living in West Texas, I can only imagine the sand as it blew upon her face.

Abraham locates the pan for the midwife. The next dilemma now kicks into place. Is it faster to run back and forth from the stream of water that flows a mile from the tent? Instantly he begins to think, "Maybe it would be better to get the mule and several pans and bring more water in one trip." "Oh, wait, before I run to get the water, I need to start a fire." Abraham's mind must have been running in a hundred different directions.

As Abraham prepares the mules to carry the water, he thinks to himself, "There has got to be an easier way than this!" He decides that after this dilemma was over he would find an easier way.

We really don't know what took place, but I promise you that if I had faced a dilemma like that I would have been trying to find water a little closer as we see below, that is what he did.

As we travel through the Old Testament, we see where Abraham, Isaac, Jacob and many other men dug wells. As the men traveled across the land, they would pick a dwelling site. They would then dig a well for their families and livestock.

Have you ever traveled to a foreign country? It always amazed me as a child as we traveled into Mexico. Living in America, I learned even the poor had an abundance of wealth. What a revelation it was to go to a land where people lived with so little or nothing at all.

DIGGING A WELL — ABRAHAM'S WELL

Once, I remember staying a week and sharing the gospel with the people there. Even as a small child it was obvious that their lives were surrounded by the love of their friends and family. Their wealth wasn't in their homes, cars, boats or clothing. They had little money but they had something that many Americans were missing.

The people in Mexico had adversity and they knew this was their way of life. No running water and floors made from dirt. The thing they had learned was to gain prosperity from their adversity. The people in this region taught their children at a young age to deal with adversity in a way that brought forth prosperity in their inner being.

Isn't this what most people are searching for? They are thinking that a new car, new house, or new mate will bring them the prosperity they are searching for. We have become a nation that is externally prosperous but internally bankrupt.

The problem with this is when your house is gone, your inner being is empty. When your car is gone, then you are broken. You are left spiritually bankrupt.

What happens to the person that has learned the prosperity of adversity? When all the wealth of this world is removed from their being, they are still prosperous. When their body is attacked, their soul is still prosperous.

And he said unto me,
My grace is sufficient for thee:
for my strength is made perfect in weakness.
Most gladly therefore will
I rather glory in my infirmities,
that the power of Christ
may rest upon me.

ABRAHAM'S WELL

> *Therefore I take pleasure in infirmities,*
> *in reproaches, in necessities,*
> *in persecutions, in distresses*
> *for Christ's sake:*
> *for when I am weak, then am I strong.*
> *II Corinthians 12:10-12*

Inspired by a sermon preached by Charles Stanley, I wrote the following poem. I thought back over my life and some of the adversities I had faced and how the Lord brought me through them. I knew my Lord was there and would carry me through.

PROSPERITY OF ADVERSITY

Prosperity of adversity is the greatest wealth of all,
To learn that whenever bad comes our way;
It's a bridge and not a wall.
The bitterness that we once had,
Was laid down at our feet.
They became the stepping stones of success
And not a path of great defeat.
The greatest servants in the world
Have learned adversity to extreme,
Learning not to focus on the hurt,
But focusing on Christ supreme.
Finding the Lord will always catch us,
No matter how far the fall.

DIGGING A WELL
ABRAHAM'S WELL

When it seems the bottom is falling out,
On the Lord is where to call.
The bridge of crossing is easier now
As we watch the waters flow.
The trials are being washed away
So that we will be free to grow.
As the time passes by, so do things
That once weighed us down,
Prosperity of adversity
Is not a weight, but a crown.

As a small child, I remember my grandfather living in Tennessee and needing a well in his back yard. He had learned the truth of the prosperity of adversity during his earlier years. His Indian heritage had taught him to "witch for wells," and he would search for the perfect branch. It had to be young and tender.

Papa Creekmore was an extremely quiet person and a man who thought things through in great depth. This was part of the Cherokee culture. Once he found the perfect branch, he would begin to walk a straight line across the property. When he walked across a location that was a good source of water, the stick would be pulled downward and would move back and forth. You could hear Granny Creekmore say, "Now won't you just look at that... beats all I ever seen!"

Depending on the pull of the stick, Papa Creekmore would then determine where he wanted to begin digging. While digging he would hit water. Again, my granny would sigh and say, "Now won't you just look at that... beats all I ever seen!"

There have been great discussions on the topic "Witching for water," is it scientific? As I was thinking about this, I could

DIGGING A WELL — ABRAHAM'S WELL

see something that the Lord would like for us to learn. The younger the branch, the easier the stick would tug toward the underground water. We are all born with a desire to search for spiritual guidance. Our children are the tender branches and they have a natural tug in their lives for "The Living Water."

When children grow older, their branches become harder. As the branches become harder, they have less pull toward the Living Water. As this happens the person begins to turn to other things to find fulfillment, instead of turning to Christ.

Mary finds her fulfillment in buying a new car. She may drive this car for a few months, but soon she begins to have another time of dissatisfaction. This time she goes out and purchases a new sofa. She is trying to fill her spiritual drawing for the Living Water with material things, instead of the Lord. This process only leads to greater dissatisfaction.

Frank has a need in his life for fulfillment. He doesn't know how to get that need met. He turns to alcohol, drugs and gambling. He keeps waking up only to find that he still has an inner need that isn't fulfilled. He turns to pornography; leading him into a greater dissatisfaction.

My son, Josh, was a staff pastor in Las Vegas, Nevada. His wife was a school teacher at one of the elementary schools. They witnessed the turmoil of children with absentee parents. There were children being left alone when most needed, throughout the night and in the early hours of the morning. All the basic things were out of order in their lives. This lifestyle causes children to start off in life drawing from the wrong aquifer.

There are thousands of children in our country today that are crying silent tears. You may not recognize these tears, as they do come in different forms. Drug abuse can be a form of silent tears. Physically "cutting" or alcoholism is another form of silent tears. Silent tears manifest themselves in many different ways stealing; lying, cheating, murder, suicide and the list goes on. All of these are ways that children cry silent tears.

What would cause so many tears to fall silently? How can we not be aware of the depth of pain and sorrow in these children's lives? There are close to three million children in our country that are experiencing these silent tears. Many of these children seem to be cared for as well as loved. Although they seem to come from wonderful homes with parents that appear to be outstanding citizens, the silent tears still fall.

We need to stop, evaluate these children's lives and see what is going on. Many are sexually abused by a family member, causing them to live in torment. Many of them have been threatened, beaten, and mentally abused.

Eventually these children fall into the trap of acceptance, never sharing their abuse and going on with life as if it never occurred. They do not talk about it because of the threats, fear or outbreaks of abuse. These children are not allowed to cry out. Yet if you listen closely, you can hear the silence of their cries.

A child that has been or is being sexually abused will start acting out. There may be outbreaks of anger. Many children start stealing, fighting and turning to drugs or alcohol to relieve the pain. Although this is not their chosen path it's one they must endure. Not being allowed to pour their hearts out, weep or even talk about this experience eats a hole in these children's lives.

Speaking with others that have cried silently for many years, I have seen the obvious pain. By the time they are grown they have learned to suppress these feelings and are unable to break free from their silence. Growing older, this destruction has eaten away at their hearts. One day they find themselves in a doctor's office, weeping, their body shaking and out of control. Medication is prescribed but what their soul really needs is to be set free.

If you have experienced sexual abuse you need to break the chain of bondage. You did not tie yourself up; nevertheless, the abuse itself put you into shackles. You have dragged those shackles to every town you've lived in, every school you have attended and you have even taken the shackles to church with you.

It is now time to get the hacksaw out and be set free! The very first step to being set free is to admit to yourself that this horrible thing has happened to you. Free yourself from guilt, shame and self blame! It was not your fault! You didn't ask for this to happen. You are not the one that needs to carry the guilt. Pull out the hacksaw and cut the chain loose. Deal with the shame and self blame. Cut the chains, let them fall and walk away! Now, you are free to move forward!

The second thing to do is absolutely the hardest. Talk to someone who is trustworthy. Share your devastation with them.

You may find yourself curled up in a ball, physically ill feeling thoughts of suicide as you open up and reveal the abuse. You may actually start throwing up.

It is normal to go through any or all of these emotions the first time you speak of the abuse. Don't stop talking. To do so would allow the chains to be re-tied to your body, weighing down your spirit to the point that you can't function.

The third thing is to continue to deal with it verbally. Seek guidance from the Lord; this will be a healing process. Verbally tell him the depth of your sorrow.

It's amazing what songs of praise can do to break the silence of tears. Christ is there for you, he longs to set you free. Scriptures on healing or comfort can also be part of the healing process. Whatever you have to do to keep moving forward, then that's what you need to do. Keeping focused on Christ, the healer is a huge part of the healing process.

Fear, being the greatest thing to overcome, is inflicted by the abuser, artificially planted by the abuser and is just a way to silence the person. This fear can be so great that the victim can't move past it. They are frozen in their steps, weeping silent tears.

> *For God hath not given*
> *us the spirit of fear;*
> *but of power, and of love,*
> *and of a sound mind.*
> *II Timothy 1:7*

Once you have admitted the abuse to someone, you can then start to move forward in your life. The following scripture will be helpful.

> *Stand fast therefore in the liberty*
> *wherewith Christ hath made us free,*
> *and be not entangled again*
> *with the yoke of bondage.*
> *Galatians 5:1*

We are to never give up on the healing process. Have you ever seen a team that walked off the field at half-time and refused to return for the second half? This would be bizarre. Even a team that is losing forty-nine to seven will keep playing until the last seconds run off the clock.

How much more exciting is the game when the team that's behind comes back after half-time! They score a touchdown

DIGGING A WELL — ABRAHAM'S WELL

and then another until finally winning the game. How shocked are the fans from both teams!

Have you ever met a person that tries to call the game in their life before it is over? They are only a quarter of the way through their life and have already given up. These people seriously need to see life for what it really is. The game is not over until the Lord calls it over.

When we start out on the journey of life we are expecting everything to go smoothly – no bumps, no bruises. I'm here to tell you, it's not going to stay that way. If you plan for bumps and bruises you will not be disappointed. They come with the journey. As we travel through this life we must learn to handle the bad things that are dealt to us, instead of quitting.

Briefly, you can take the time to think about the bad things. Dwelling too long can cause the shackles to reattach themselves to your body.

Life goes on even if you choose not to. Other people keep moving, changing, growing and succeeding. The only way for you to do the same is to get into the game.

There are too many players that are still in the locker room, sitting on the bench and dwelling on the things that went wrong in their childhood. They are locked in the past – unable to move forward. They are blaming everyone, including their coaches, for their pain.

Half-time is over and the whistle has been blown, it's time to play ball. Get off the bench and walk back onto the field! Get your eyes on the clock that is running instead of the time wasted in the first half of your life.

Until the game is over in your life, don't call off the game. Let the Lord be the one to call the final play. Keep your eyes on him. It's the only way to complete the game of life.

CHAPTER FOUR

BITTER WATER OF MARAH

*Now when they came to Marah,
they could not drink the waters
of Marah, for they were bitter.
Therefore the name of it
was called Marah
Exodus 16:23*

There are many places, even some mentioned in the scripture, where you would not want to dig your well. The water at Marah is the very place that nobody desires to stop and dig a well for their family to drink. Although, many times

DIGGING A WELL: BITTER WATER OF MARAH

that's the very place we find ourselves digging.

Passing through the desert lands, the Israelites would go days without water. One can only imagine what it would be like to be traveling through the dry barren land and not have water to quench their thirst. Looking far into the distance someone spots water. Hurriedly they move towards the water, only to find that this water is not good for drinking. This water is bitter. There are many places in this region with bodies of water that are bitter. There is the Great Bitter Lake, Little Bitter Lake and then there is Marah. In our lives we will be given the opportunity to drink from trials of bitterness.

Everyone reading this has probably at one time or another been offered the water of Marah. Did you drink from it when it was offered?

When the Israelites came to the water, they had a choice, to trust God or become bitter. Needless to say, they chose what you and I probably would have chosen–grumbling and complaining.

Turning to God Moses asked, "What should I do?"

Now why did the Israelites not turn to Moses? They could have asked Moses to stop and pray to the Lord God Almighty. God had just parted the Red Sea and let them go across on dry land. Maybe for the same reasons we do not– lack of faith. We should stop and pray and ask for the Lord's guidance.

God can carry us through a trial and we are praising his name all the way through it. During this trial we have no grumbles or complaints. However, we might not be so full of praise during the next trial. Our mouths are filled with skepticism, revealing our lack of faith. Do you find yourself being like the Israelites when faced with difficult times?

God knew before the Israelites ever came to Marah that they would be passing through that way. He had already made prior arrangements for his children. By the waters of Marah, a tree was growing.

Many years prior to their arrival, God had allowed a seed to fall to the ground and germinate. The tree stood by the waters, waiting for the Israelites to pass by. Moses turned to God and asked, "What should I do?" God showed Moses a tree.

> *"And when they came to Marah,*
> *they could not drink of the*
> *waters of Marah for they were bitter:*
> *therefore the name of it was called Marah.*
> *And the people murmured*
> *against Moses, saying,*
> *"What shall we drink?"*
> *And he cried unto the Lord,*
> *and the Lord showed him a tree,*
> *which when he had cast into the waters,*
> *the waters were made sweet."*
> *Exodus 15:23-25*

There's actually a tree called the Moringa Oleifera tree.[1] This tree is known to purify bad water[2]. We don't know if this is the type of tree that the Lord had allowed to germinate beside the waters of Marah. We do know that the Lord was the one that showed the tree to Moses when he prayed.

The Lord has provided a Moringa Oleifera tree, cleansing from bitterness. Whenever you pass through the bitter stages of

---

[1] http://www.naturalnes.com/022272_Moringa_medical_herbs.html
[2] http://www.youtube.com/watch?v=KqPBmERC7OU

DIGGING A WELL — BITTER WATER OF MARAH

life, know that the tree provided for you is the cross. He has provided what you need. Just turn to him and ask. Don't choose to grumble and complain!

Be a Moses! Turn to God and ask for the Lord to show you how to turn your bitter water into sweet.

God may use a friend or family member to help you find this tree. It may be an item he may use or a book. Just ask the Lord and he will show you how to turn your bitterness into the joy of the Lord.

As the Lord was to the Israelites, their Jehovah-Rapha, ("the God that healeth thee"), he can also be your Jehovah-Rapha.

Our children, grandchildren, friends and acquaintances will be drinking from the waters where we drink. Do not dig your well too close to the Great Bitter Lakes or Marah.

Digging too close to Marah and the Great Bitter Lakes will cause your well to flow with bitterness. Dig as close to the River of Life as possible. (We'll discuss this in chapter eight). Then you will know that the water your family drinks from is the Living Water.

Pick up the newspapers in any city. You can read story after story of people who have chosen to drink the water at Marah. Let's just look at a few examples of what drove people to drink from the bitter water.

> Lane was "a quiet kid. Freshman year he got into a 'goth' phase and didn't talk to that many people anymore. He never egged anybody on. He just went about his business." But Lane's family life had been disrupted by divorce and violence. His parents divorced in 2002, and his father later served time in jail on assault and other charges, according to the station.
>
> Classmates described Lane as an outcast who'd been

bullied. In late December he posted a poem on his Facebook page that read: "He longed for only one thing, the world to bow at his feet," and ended ominously: "Die, all of you."

Lane allegedly opened fire with a handgun just slighly before 8 a.m. in the school cafeteria where students were eating breakfast.[3]

Another article states:

Many serial killers have faced similar problems in their childhood development. Hickey's Trauma Control Model explains how early childhood trauma can set the child up for deviant behavior in adulthood. The child's environment (either their parents or society) is the dominant factor in whether or not the child's behavior escalates into homicidal activity.

Family, or lack thereof, is the most prominent part of a child's development because it is what the child can identify with on a regular basis. "The serial killer is no different than any other individual who is instigated to seek approval from parents, sexual partners, or others." This need for approval is what influences children to attempt to develop social relationships with their family and peers, but if they are rejected or neglected, they are unable to do so. This results in the lowering of their self-esteem and helps develop their fantasy world in which they are in control. Hickey's Trauma Control Model clearly shows that the development of a serial killer is based on an early trauma followed by facilitators (porn, drugs, and alcohol) and disposition (the inability to attach).

Family interaction also plays an important role in a

---

[3] http://abcnews.go.com/US/ohio-high-school-shooting-prosecuters-tj-lane-adult/story?id=15814303&page=2

child's growth and development. "The quality of their attachments to parents and other members of the family are critical to how these children relate to and value other members of society.

Wilson and Seaman (1990) conducted a study on incarcerated serial killers and what they felt was the most influential factor that contributed to their homicidal activity. Almost all of the serial killers in the study had experienced some sort of environmental problems during their childhood, such as a broken home, or a lack of discipline in the home. It was common for the serial killers to come from a family that had experienced divorce, separation, or the lack of a parent. Furthermore, nearly half of the serial killers had experienced some type of physical and sexual abuse and even more had experienced emotional neglect. When a parent has a drug or alcohol problem, the attention in the household is on the parents rather than the child. This neglect of the child leads to the lowering of their self-esteem and helps develop a fantasy world in which they are in control. Hickey's Trauma Control Model supports how the neglect from parents can facilitate deviant behavior especially if the child sees substance abuse in action. This then leads to disposition (the inability to attach), which can further lead to homicidal behavior unless the child finds a way to develop substantial relationships and fight the label they receive. If a child receives support from those around him or her, then he or she is unlikely to recover from the traumatic event in a positive way. As stated by E. E. Maccoby, "the family has continued to be seen as a major—perhaps the major—arena for socialization".[4]

---

[4] http://en,wikipedia.org/wiki/serial_killer

DIGGING A WELL — BITTER WATER OF MARAH

We also read:

Co-occurring disorders are grave and often lead teens to consider suicide.

During the despair and suffering of depression, many teens seriously consider ending their young lives. When they add alcohol or drugs to the mix, all too often the results are life-altering and even fatal.

Studies indicate that alcohol and drug abuse are second only to depression and other mood disorders as the most frequent risk factors for suicide.

Statistics gathered show—

- 20 percent of teens seriously consider suicide.
- 14 percent of teens have made a suicide plan.
- 8 percent of teens make a suicide attempt.
- 70 percent of youth who make a suicide attempt are frequent alcohol and/or drug users.
- Binge drinking significantly increases suicidal ideation, planning and attempts[5]

We see that our world is filled with bitter water. Oh, that we could just put a seal on this well!

There is not just one body of water called Marah. The scripture says in Exodus 15 that the Israelites stopped at the "waters" (plural) of Marah.

If there was just one bitter well that Satan put in our world, we probably could cap it; although, the moment we put a cap on one, we turn around and there is another one. Do you ever feel you are just surrounded by waters of Marah?

---

[5] http://www.speaneohio.org/about-teen-suicide-and-depression/adolescent-depression-and-substance-abuse

DIGGING A WELL
BITTER WATER OF MARAH

We especially do not want to see our children and loved ones drinking from the bitter water of Marah. Yet, daily we see people turning to it.

Is it only the lost world that turns to these waters? No, we read in the newspapers, hear on the radio and see on television of Christians drinking from Marah instead of turning to the Living Water.

Oh, what devastation this can bring! Just because we have the best aquifer doesn't mean that we are exempt from drinking bitter water.

My dear mother, at the age of forty-four, decided to visit the Well at Marah. The water at Marah didn't only poison her life, but poisoned lives for generations. Late one evening, deciding she was no longer happy or useful to anyone, she shot herself.

If I could, I would have given anything to be there and say, "Mom, please don't drink the water, it has poison!"

The poison began to eat away at our family. There was only one way to put a stop to our bitterness and that was by turning to the Living Water.

There have been times when I would get discouraged and begin walking back to the waters of Marah. Thinking back, I am reminded that the bitter waters at Marah will affect my family for generations to come, just as my mother's did me.

Since I have been taken to the water at Marah, I need to turn to the Lord and ask him to show me what can make this water in my life sweet.

If your family has been taken to this well, you might have to write out a decree and get family members to sign it. You might want to use the "DECLARATION OF LIFE" that I've written out on the following page.

DIGGING A WELL | **BITTER WATER OF MARAH**

DECLARATION OF LIFE

I declare on this date, _____, I, _____, will never drink from the Well of Destruction and take my own life or the life of any human being.

I, _____, will seek guidance from a counselor, pastor or doctor if I ever feel that taking my own life is an option.

I refuse to listen to the voice of defeat that is trying to destroy my life.

I, _____, declare on this day, that I will live my life for the Lord. I will watch, obey his guidance, serve and help others to be strong and not be defeated.

Signed_____
Date _____

Witnesses _____
_____

DIGGING A WELL
BITTER WATER OF MARAH

Mentally, I signed this decree many times, seeing the last sentence as being very important. Had I listened to the voice my mother listened to, I would not be writing songs or this book.

What has she missed out on in life due to drinking from the waters of Marah? She missed cherished times with her children and grandchildren. All it took was one sip and she vanished.

Our daughter, Lisa Joy, has been given many opportunities to drink from this well. Each time I see her on the brink and see the cup about to touch her lips, she softly reminds herself that the water from this well only brings more sorrow.

After birth, she became very ill. As I watched the nurses poke Lisa and listened to her cry of despair, I just couldn't believe they were doing this to my little baby. After four hours of trying to locate a vein in her little body, they turned to me and said, "We have no choice. We are going to have to try to get this IV into her head."

To this day, when I think about this, I get sick at my stomach. I remember standing out in the hall and calling Steve on the phone and telling him I didn't think I could cope with it. We began to pray and during this prayer, I took a deep breath and realized I needed to be strong. After all, I wasn't the one being poked, I was just the mother. Lisa was the one suffering from the needles being inserted by the nurses.

Once the IV was properly placed into her head, it didn't take long before she regained her strength. Following pneumonia, she began a series of medical difficulties lasting a lifetime.

Allergic to almost everything, Lisa at one point had to have her hair cut short. Every time it touched her soft delicate skin she would break out in welts.

I remember when she looked into the mirror after the

hairdresser had cut it shorter than requested. After taking one look, Lisa turned to the hairdresser and said, "You dumb dumb head!"

Hitting her teenage years, Lisa realized that the medications had taken a toll on her body. Several times she went to bed with a toothache. Waking up the next morning, she would look like someone had slammed the side of her face with a baseball bat. We would have to call and make an appointment for a root canal.

Little did we realize that in her journey of life, she would go through so many sorrows. You can't have great strength, without great resistance.

The Lord knew Lisa Joy would have to be our strong-willed child just to make it through all the things she would face. She needed every bit of this strong will she could get in order to survive.

Entering college, other things began to manifest themselves in her body. During her second year of college she had to drop out, return home and spend many months unable to do anything. She was tested for Lupus, Crohn's Disease, and numerous other diseases. The doctors could never pinpoint what was wrong.

I remember the day Dr. West of Lubbock sat down with us and said, "We don't have the answers. All we know is her body has rejected her colon and it has to be removed."

To Lisa, this would be like saying she's no good anymore, worthless, and will not amount to anything.

The days, weeks and months that followed were extremely trying as I watched her walk up to the Well of Marah. She would say, "I have the right to drink from this well! Life has dealt me a lemon." She and I had many conversations about her illnesses. My response to her was, "I agree, life has dealt you a

DIGGING A WELL
BITTER WATER OF MARAH

lemon. It's time to make lemonade."

I went on to say, "Lisa, pull through it and someday you can hold someone else's hand that has to walk this path. Give up, accomplish nothing, and drink from that bitter well. If you do, who do you think will get the glory?"

After six surgeries in one year, I walked into her room. She was writing a book. During the next few months she poured herself into the pages and when she finished, she had compiled a book for children. So much of her life was tucked away and hidden in the stories of the book.

What had taken place as she was writing? She exchanged the "I" from the word (bitter) and replaced it with an "E" for (better).

Was this the last of her trials? No, she has had many more trials – to the point that I thought it would rip her heart out!

I watched as she walked to the bitter well. She would start to sip, but hesitate. Pondering on her grandmother's choice and what her mother had taught her caused her to turn from the bitter water.

This doesn't mean that she didn't sit there for awhile. I believe that we all sit there for a moment or two. Then we have to decide what we are going to do – get bitter, or get better.

| DIGGING A WELL | WELL OF SALVATION |

CHAPTER FIVE

WELL OF SALVATION

*Nevertheless a lad saw them,
and told Absalom:
but they went both of
them away quickly,
and came to a man's
house in Bahurim,
which had a well in his court;
whither they went down.
And the woman took and spread a
covering over the well's mouth,*

DIGGING A WELL — WELL OF SALVATION

*and spread ground corn thereon;
and the thing was not known.
And when Absalom's servants
came to the woman to the house,
they said, Where is Ahimaaz and
Jonathan? And the woman
said unto them, they be gone
over the brook of water.
And when they had sought
and could not find them, they
returned to Jerusalem.
II Samuel 17:18-20*

The Lord chooses to use the most unusual things to protect us. Would you, like this woman, have thought to spread a covering over the well? Would you have thought to tell the men, "Climb into the well?" Would you have thought to spread corn on top of the covering? The very act that this woman chose was the act that would save their lives.

You may find yourself in a situation, as I did, where God puts someone before you to literally save that person's life. In doing so, they may come to the saving knowledge of the Lord Jesus Christ through your touch.

While working at the Baptist Student Center, a young lady came to me and said, "Sherry, I have a friend that I need you to talk to. Will you take time and meet with her?"

There was pain in her eyes as she told me her friend's name. What I was seeing was no ordinary pain. It was not the pain of losing a boyfriend or failing a class. It was much deeper.

DIGGING A WELL OF SALVATION

She said this young girl (we'll call her Amanda) was scheduled to have an abortion at 3:30 p.m. that day. She wanted me to help change her friend's mind. She had spoken with her earlier that day, but couldn't convince her to change her mind.

If her best friend was unable to change her mind, how could I possibly persuade her? Agreeing to talk with her, my next question was, "What will I say – what will I do? This is much bigger than I am!"

As Amanda walked into my office and slid into the chair, I remember the sad, distant look on her face. I began to ask questions and share my beliefs in the Lord with her. Stating that I believed abortions are wrong. I shared a pamphlet of the procedure with her. After going over the pamphlet, she still had that determined look on her face.

Jeff Ford, the Baptist Student Director, was in his office. I slipped away from Amanda for a moment. I asked Jeff if he had a medical replica of a baby during the different stages of the pregnancy. He handed me the little models. I carried them into my office and placed them into Amanda's hand thinking, "Now this will be the determining factor of this baby's life!" But it wasn't.

It was time for Amanda to call her boyfriend to pick her up. They would drive together to the abortion clinic and terminate the pregnancy. She had previously explained that she and her boyfriend had already discussed it. In agreement, they would not raise their children in poverty.

As Amanda was walking out of my office, my eye caught the prayer room down the hall. We had just prayed but I was wondering if what I was feeling was correct. The tugging would not leave my heart.

"Amanda," I quickly said, "before you leave, let's go into

DIGGING A WELL OF SALVATION

the prayer room. Let me pray for you and the doctor that will be doing the procedure."

She agreed and as we walked into the prayer room I felt the Lord leading me to ask Amanda to sit in the rocking chair.

It seemed out of place that someone had placed a rocking chair in the corner of the prayer room. It was God's divine intervention that Amanda would sit in this particular rocking chair. Ironically, this was the type of chair a mother would sit in to rock her baby.

As Amanda sat down, I felt the Lord lead me to kneel at her feet. Not understanding why, I lowered myself before her and took her hands in mine. Looking into her eyes I requested that she envision me as her mother.

Now I asked softly, "Amanda, what would you say to your mother?"

The moment I said this, Amanda fell out of the chair and into my arms. She began asking forgiveness from her mother.

She said, "Mommy, I love this little baby and I would never take its life! Please forgive me! I'm so sorry! I want to raise this baby; I just can't! I have no money. I don't have a job. There is no way I could feed this baby. I feel my only choice is to have an abortion!"

That very day Amanda felt the hand of God touch her life.

For the previous five years I had been working on a baby blanket. When the weather was bad, I would take it out and work on it for awhile. The only thing I lacked was putting the hand-stitched hem on a corner.

Leaving my house early that morning, I had put the blanket into my car thinking I would complete it during lunch.

My own children had asked several times who the blanket was for. I would tell them that it was probably for one of my future grandbabies, but honestly I was uncertain whom it was for.

The Lord knew before I even cut the first square for the blanket exactly whose name would be on it. He knows every detail of your life, even how many hairs you have on your head. He knows what you have done in the past and what you will do in the future.

God knows all the hidden secrets that are buried so deep in one's heart. They are tucked safely away so nobody can find them. They are buried so deep that one has forgotten they are hidden there. Jesus Christ may knock softly at the door and say, "Let me inside this room."

One's response might be "Oh no, Lord, not this room. That's the place in my heart that no one goes. There are too many things hidden inside that nobody knows about but me."

He looks softly at you and says, "I want to make you clean but first I must enter into this forbidden place."

He is not a God that barges in and does spring cleaning without permission. He doesn't go in and burn the room down. The Lord softly walks through the room and places the items into your hands. He lets you decide what will stay and what will be thrown out.

At the end of this purifying process, we are surprised at the items we had held on to. These items will no longer dwell in the secret place. [6]

Immediately, the awesome feeling of cleansing sweeps over us. There is now the feeling of having a place to store new things, good things, such as songs and scriptures. Now instead of all the secret things that had gathered dirt and cobwebs, we have things such as joy, contentment, and peace.

---

[6] This concept was borrowed from the song "Secret Place" by Steve and Annie Chapman.

DIGGING A WELL: WELL OF SALVATION

You see, Jesus has set you free. You may be in chains of bondage; however, "Those chains are not holding you. You are the one holding the chains."[7] You have been hiding them in the secret compartment of your heart, hoping nobody will ever see. They have been weighing you down, keeping you from moving forward with the Lord.

Refreshed and anew is the way that Amanda felt as we went to the Lord in prayer. When she allowed the heavenly Father to walk into her secret place, it was replaced with courage, hope, love and compassion. She was given a peace that passes all understanding.

After closing in prayer I asked Amanda to stay in the prayer room. I went out to my car and picked up the baby blanket. I told the Lord, "Thank you for allowing me to listen to your voice to sew this blanket. Thank you, Lord, for touching my heart this morning, for guiding me to bring this blanket to work."

As I carried the blanket into the room, Amanda began to weep. She began to say, "If God can send a new blanket on the very day I chose to keep my baby, then I am confident that he will feed and clothe this child for me."

I watched as Amanda stood, squared her shoulders and left my office with assurance and confidence. She felt that her heavenly Father loved her as much as he loved anybody else. Obviously, he had saved her baby's life and gave that child a special gift, all within a few hours.

It has been about thirteen years since that day and I have received pictures of her precious teenager. This teen is growing into a fine young adult. Amanda shared with me the joy of getting to hear her child's laughter while running and splashing in the ocean.

---

[7] Quote from Beth Moore video: Here and Now, There and Then.

DIGGING A WELL — WELL OF SALVATION

Amanda married the young man that was the child's father. Today, he stands with his arm around his son, his pride and joy. He feels grateful that Amanda did not honor his request. This man is blessed to have his son to be a part of his life.

Your well may be a Well of Salvation in a different way. Turn to the Lord and ask him to tug at the hearts of people in your path. Ask him to use you to guide them to the living water. As they drink from the Well of Salvation, it may keep them from alcohol, drug abuse or suicide. It could even save a life.

> *"If any man thirst, let him*
> *come unto me, and drink."*
> *John 7:37*

He didn't say "Sip from the well" he said "Drink." Come and let it soak into your mouth, wet your throat and run through your veins. Absorb it,

> *"O taste and see that*
> *the Lord is good".*
> *Psalm 34.8*

The story above and the following story remind me of a scripture in the word of God, where it says:

> *"And I will pray the Father,*
> *and he shall give you*
> *another Comforter, that he may*
> *abide with you for ever".*
> *John 14:16*

| DIGGING A WELL | WELL OF SALVATION |

There are two different stories here, one above and the one shown below. Both of these stories talk about a blanket, a perfect example of how the heavenly Father cares for us.

In John Chapter fourteen, God says he will give us a comforter. He isn't saying that he is going to send us a new blanket. He is speaking of the Holy Spirit, who watches over, protects, leads, guides, and yes, comforts us.

Stephanie Becker found herself at this very well on March 2, 2012.

> She lived in a quant town in Indiana that sits in the heart of the rolling hills in Henryville, Indiana.
>
> The warning had been sounded in the mid-afternoon. The news station had predicted severe weather. School had been dismissed early.
>
> Stephanie's day started out just like an ordinary day in Henryville Indiana, living in her dream home with her husband and two beautiful children. Dominic and Rose had placed their handprints into the cement, marking that this house belonged to the Decker family.
>
> Today things were going to change that would impact their family for the rest of their lives.
>
> When the children in Henryville woke up that morning the furthest thing from their minds was that today they might not live to see another day, that they may never see their mother again, that they may never play with their neighbor friends again, that they would not have a home to live in, a car to drive or their favorite toys. They had no idea that the sky would turn from a glorious blue into a horrific dark gray in such a short period of time.
>
> As Stephanie watched the storm brewing, she realized things were getting out of hand. She grabbed

DIGGING A WELL — WELL OF SALVATION

her two precious children and headed for the basement. On the way down she grabbed a comforter and threw it over the children. Looking above, she could see the house being torn into rubbish, glass flying, beams being ripped off the structure of the home. She flung her body on top of her two children, not knowing what would happen next.

Suddenly there was the calm before the real storm was to hit. Little did Stephanie know, but in order to save the lives of these precious children she had jeopardized her very life during the worst part of the storm. She slowly uncovered her children and used the comforter as a tourniquet for her legs. She didn't know what the injuries were at this point; she just knew she was bleeding.

"Dominic, run get the neighbors, Mommy needs help!" After doctors and nurses extensively ministered to Stephanie, it was decided she would have to undergo a double amputation.[8]

As I watched this story on ABC, I would glance up occasionally and give it half my attention. That was, until they were interviewing the family and said that everyone was devastated at what Stephanie's reaction would be when she awakened to find that both legs had to be amputated.

In fear, they stood waiting for the moment of reaction. To their surprise, when Stephanie was told what had taken place, she took a deep breath and said, "Well it looks like there will be no more pedicures for me," and then chuckled.

At that moment the ice broke for the whole family. Everyone was able to relax, breath, and know Stephanie was going to be OK.

---

[8] Abcnews.com

DIGGING A WELL — WELL OF SALVATION

Not only had Stephanie visited the Well of Salvation that day, she had walked right past the Well of Marah. She obviously had decided she wanted no part of that well. You see, "the well" she would drink from would be a well for her precious children to draw from. They would learn firsthand how to have joy in the mist of destruction.

I wanted to tell you about Stephanie because I knew her story was one that would be encouraging to others who found themselves faced with the question, "What well am I going to drink from when I face hardship"?

Letters have been written to the National Weather Station expressing how wonderful it is to have them in place to give us warning of these events.

Our heavenly Father has also set up a Weather Station for each of us. He has been tenderly, patiently and consistently sounding the alarm. This alarm has been sounded for centuries.

He had men write it on stone, sound it from the rooftops, spend their entire lives warning people of the destruction to come. He has never failed us on his promises.

Stephanie was wise enough to gather her two children, take them into a basement, then cover them with a comforter. She placed her own body on top of their bodies so they would be protected. Our heavenly Father has done the same for us.

> *"Howl ye; for the day of the LORD*
> *is at hand; it shall come as a*
> *destruction from the Almighty.*
> *Therefore shall all hands be faint,*
> *and every man's heart shall melt:*
> *And they shall be afraid:*
> *pangs and sorrows*

> *shall take hold of them;*
> *they shall be in pain*
> *as a woman that travaileth:*
> *they shall be amazed one at another;*
> *their faces shall be as flames.*
> *Behold, the day of the LORD cometh,*
> *cruel both with wrath*
> *and fierce anger,*
> *to lay the land desolate:*
> *and he shall destroy*
> *the sinners thereof out of it.*
> *For the stars of heaven*
> *and the constellations*
> *thereof shall not give their light:*
> *the sun shall be darkened*
> *in his going forth,*
> *and the moon shall not cause*
> *her light to shine.*
> *And I will punish the*
> *world for their evil,*
> *and the wicked for their iniquity;*
> *and I will cause the arrogancy*
> *of the proud to cease,*
> *and will lay low the*
> *haughtiness of the terrible."*
> *Isaiah 13:6-11*

The Lord sounded the alarm! The Lord gave the forecast of

| DIGGING A WELL | WELL OF SALVATION |

that day! It will be stronger and do more destruction than any F4 or F5 tornado. He has asked you and me to help him get the news to everyone.

> *The great day of the LORD is near,*
> *it is near, and hasteth greatly,*
> *even the voice of the LORD:*
> *the mighty man shall*
> *cry there bitterly.*
> *Zephaniah 1:14*

When the weather alarm goes off, do we heed its warning or just ignore it? Jesus has sent his Comforter as well as sounding the alarm.

There is coming a day when we all shall kneel before him and give an account of our lives. What well will you be able to say that you drank from? What well did you dig for other people?

Oh, that we might all drink from the Well of Salvation. That we might lead others to taste and see that the Lord is good! His mercies endure forever!

Isn't it amazing how the Lord sends people into our lives? He wants to use us in an inspiring way. There have been times that God moved in a way that allowed me to know it was a "God thing."

The following is a true story; names have been changed to protect their identity.

The elementary Sunday School teacher was ill one particular Sunday. My class had no students on this Sunday. I was taking my enrollment book to the office and noticed this class' teacher was missing. I really didn't have a lesson

DIGGING A WELL — WELL OF SALVATION

prepared for that age group but the Lord knew I was not going to be teaching that morning.

Ivan and Julie are brother and sister. I started the class with small talk, asking them if they had lived in our town all their lives.

Ivan took a deep breath and said, "All our lives except for a little while."

Ivan stated, "Our father is in prison!"

Not really knowing what to say, I replied, "Oh, I'm sorry, are you are living with your mom?"

Ivan's eyes saddened. "No, our mom lives about a hundred miles away." My heart broke for these two children. You could see the pain on their faces as they spoke.

Julie looked me straight in the eyes, took a deep breath and stated, "When our Dad went to prison I was really mad!"

She explained that they had to move to North Dakota and live with their Aunt Mary. "We hated her and would scream at her and tell her we didn't want to live with her.

But you know what? We wouldn't know what we would do now if we had not moved to Mary's house."

Waiting for more of the heartbreaking story I wondered if the conversation should be cut off. I was thinking that I should begin teaching the lesson to these children. These two obviously needed to hear about Jesus and how he can change their lives.

Quietly I began praying and asking, "Lord, what lesson should I pull out of my hat and teach?"

Julie kept on talking about their moving to Mary's. She went on to say because of "this," she now knows about a certain thing (not explaining what "this" was). She took a deep breath and I could see excitement in her eyes.

DIGGING A WELL — WELL OF SALVATION

This spurred me to ask her, "Julie, just what did you learn at Mary's house?"

She smiled the biggest smile and said, "We learned about Jesus." ("This," being Jesus,)

Cold chills began to run all over me as I could hear the love in her voice when she said the name of Jesus.

Ivan chimed in, "Yes, we learned about Jesus."

Anyone could have felt that this was not just a normal experience but they had truly met the Lord Jesus Christ. It was plain to see he had transformed their lives. The love for this new found friend was radiating through his life.

Eager to hear a little child's view of learning about Jesus, I then decided that a lesson would not be pulled out of my hat.

Julie began to tell just what Jesus had meant in her life. She explained that all her family– aunts, uncles, cousins, mom, dad and everybody in their family drank alcohol. As they explained, it was obvious that they didn't just drink but their lives were truly consumed by it.

The pain was so plain to see on both of the children's faces, especially on Ivan's. There was deep pain as he lowered his head.

Ivan said, "Yes, Julie is right, but at Mary's house it was different. Mary is like a missionary who years ago had met Joey. Joey is part of my dad's family that drinks all the time. Joey learned about Jesus, and now his life is different than everyone else in the family. He's really nice and everyone else is mean."

Ivan began to take over the conversation with a smile. "Would you like to hear what Jesus did in our lives?"

I listened with the utmost attention. These two children must have really experienced salvation in Jesus Christ.

Ivan shook his head and said, "Julie used to have marks all over her body all the time."

My heart broke as pictures started formulating into my mind of how her parents must have been the ones abusing her.

Julie broke into the conversation with, "Ivan used to pinch me until I would bleed every day. He would come into my bedroom, bite me and beat my face until my eye turned purple." Ivan was very mean to me.

Ivan broke in: "Yes, but I don't do that anymore." Ivan looked me in the face and you could see peace move across his expression. Emotions filled me in such a way that I can't explain.

Julie interrupted, "Ivan, tell the teacher what you do now instead of leaving marks all over my body."

My eyes were filled with tears as I realized these two children didn't just meet Jesus Christ, they were asking Jesus to walk with, embrace and help them. They wanted to show other people about this person they had met that could change a horrible angry child into someone that could love, care for and help others.

Julie broke in once again, "Tell her Ivan, tell her, what you do now that Jesus lives in our hearts."

Ivan opened his Bible, looked at Julie with compassion and said, "Each night this Bible goes with me into Julie's bedroom and I read to Julie what it says."

Julie chided in, "And you know what? Every time he reads to me he colors the words that he has read with a yellow highlighter."

Ivan opened his bible and began to turn the pages in it. The Bible was covered with yellow highlights.

They shared how they moved back to their hometown and

now live with family members. They found our church and wanted to come and learn more.

Pray for us as we minister to these two young children. Oh, how they blessed me! I am so thankful for the opportunity I had to meet these two living testimonies.

A couple years have passed since that Sunday morning. Our church has been forever changed. There were several events taking place at that time. These events changed the flow of the well at our church. In a later chapter I will explain some miracles that have occurred since this event took place.

CHAPTER SIX

WHAT STOPS YOUR WELL?

And ye shall smite every fenced city, and every choice city, and shall fell every good tree, and stop all wells of water, and mar every good piece of land with stones.
II Kings 3:19

What causes your well to stop flowing? Earthquakes can. What earthquakes have you experienced lately that have changed or stopped the flow of your well?

The passage in II Kings refers to the practice of ancient armies which would "stop all wells of water" in order to help

DIGGING A WELL — WHAT STOPS YOUR WELL?

them defeat their enemies. Cutting the water source can be part of destroying a city.

This is true in our lives. We are in constant need of the Living Water. Too many times we are not willing to drink from the word of God. Therefore, our lives are like the well, which becomes stagnant when the water stops.

Have you experienced failure or pain in your life? If you are alive and old enough to read this book, then your answer is probably, "Yes." Failure and pain are a part of each of our lives. It's the part of our lives that we don't enjoy, but it's also a part of our lives that makes us stronger.

Thomas Edison could tell you many stories about failure.[9] The only way to succeed is by falling down and then getting back up. There were people in Thomas Edison's life that believed he would never succeed. His school teacher said there was something wrong with him so his parents took him out of school. Other than the first three months of his schooling, he was educated only by his parents.

Edison became well-known after he perfected the light bulb that Humphrey Davy invented. Later he flipped a switch that sent light into eighty-five homes in New York. He also invented the phonograph, electric mixers, motion picture camera, and numerous other things.

At the age of eighty-four, Thomas Edison passed away known as the greatest inventor of all time, with 1,093 inventions.

Edwin Howard Armstrong[10] was much like Thomas Edison. He had been removed from the public school and became withdrawn, at which time his interest in electrical and mechanic devices increased.

---

[9] http://gardenofpraise.com/ibdediso.htm
[10] http://radioworld.comDefault.aspx?tabid=64&ArticleID=185047

DIGGING A WELL — WHAT STOPS YOUR WELL?

Edwin built a tower in his backyard at a very young age. At twenty-one he entered the U.S. Army Signal Corps. He set up wireless communications for the army during that time. He allowed the Army to use many of his patents.

This young man went on to invent numerous things that we use every day. In 1934 RCA hired Edwin to conduct the first large scale field test for FM radio. This test was conducted by putting an antenna on the eighty-fifth floor of the Empire State Building. There were people eighty-five miles away that could pick up the signal.

In 1935 Edwin financed construction of the first FM radio station, W2XMN. The signal could be heard for one hundred miles. The tower was located in Alpine, New Jersey.

RCA began to lobby against FM radio. They chose to move forward with broadcasting television. They didn't want to be dominated by FM radio. When this took place, Edwin charged RCA and NBC with infringement.

The event with RCA and NBC began a bitter legal battle for Edwin that lasted twelve years. Edwin was also involved in many other legal battles. These battles took about ninety percent of his time, leaving him with little money, exhausted and frustrated.

On January 31, 1954, Edwin took his own life by jumping out the window of his thirteenth floor apartment.

His wife began to fight the legal battles after the death of Edwin and was able to get patents on his inventions.

On September 11, 2001, when planes struck the twin towers and the towers fell, all communications were lost for eight major TV stations in New York. All radio towers had been placed on top of the Twin Towers. Without the ability to communicate and share with America what was happening, New York would be lost and alone.

DIGGING A WELL

WHAT STOPS YOUR WELL?

America was under attack and TV executives were looking for somewhere to turn. Someone remembered about the tower that Edwin Armstrong had built in 1935. It was still on the Empire State Building. Authorities were contacted and reminded that the tower was still there. It was then turned on and communication with America was restored.

In his own defeat, this man committed suicide. Fifty-eight years later, on September 11, 2001, he was a major reason America was set back on its feet.

Never give up. Even when you feel your life is worthless, you never know what God has in store for you.

> *My brethren, count it all joy*
> *when ye fall into divers temptations;*
> *Knowing this, that the*
> *trying of your faith worketh patience.*
> *But let patience have her*
> *perfect work, that ye may be*
> *perfect and entire,*
> *wanting nothing.*
> *If any of you lack wisdom,*
> *let him ask of God, that*
> *giveth to all men liberally,*
> *and upbraideth not;*
> *and it shall be given him.*
> *But let him ask in faith,*
> *nothing wavering.*
> *For he that wavereth*
> *is like a wave*

WHAT STOPS YOUR WELL?

of the sea driven with
the wind and tossed.
James 1:2-6

In my dedication of this book, I told how God, through unusual means, took me to the Guadalupe Mountains. At this point, I must tell you what happened there. This was the day that I was supposed to start writing this book.

After arriving at the mountains, I began to pack water and snacks for the youth group's four hour hike. Soon the realization that things were not going as planned set in. My daughter, Lisa, had decided to stay at the bottom of the mountain with me. At the time I felt it would be a distraction, as I wanted to begin my writings.

It was uncomfortable sitting inside a pickup truck, trying to write a book. The weather turned colder than expected. Because of this, I was unable to sit at the picnic table to behold the beauty of the mountains while writing.

Unknown to me, on the two-hour trip to the mountains the computer's battery had died. Opening the cover to the laptop, I turned the computer on, but nothing happened. Sitting there with a black screen, you would have thought that I would have been a bit disappointed. Not me, I was off the hook! This would make it easy to tell Jonean that I misunderstood the Lord. Obviously, God really did not want me to write this book. If he did, my computer would not have a black screen at this point.

This is where I was reminded that my ways are not the Lord's ways. Realizing that the Lord had allowed Lisa to stay at the foot of the mountains, she wasn't a distraction at all. She was a blessing. God was going to use her in a mighty way.

While packing the computer supplies back into the bag, I

DIGGING A WELL
WHAT STOPS YOUR WELL?

heard Lisa say, "Hey Mom, there are some bathrooms right up the hill." I'm thinking, "Whooptee doo!"

Then she said, "Why don't you walk up there and see if there is a power supply to plug your laptop into."

Out of the truck, with laptop and power cord in hand, I entered into the ladies' bathroom. There was no power plug to be seen. As I left the bathroom, I searched around the building for a power plug. There were none to be found. Once again, I was off the hook!

As I started walking away from the building, a man walked up to me. He looked at me puzzled and said, "Ma'am what are you doing with a laptop in the mountains? Most people come up here to get away from laptops, cell phones, and the hustle and bustle."

"I came to the mountains to write a book, I said." As these words left my lips I felt so silly. I was thinking, "Me, little ole me, planning on writing a book?"

This gentleman's name was Michael Haynie. He asked, "What is your book about?"

I stated, "Digging a Well. I've come here to research and write about wells."

I was planning on using my computer to do most of the research. The Lord had other plans. He had placed me right in the path of Michael, the one who could answer many questions for Lisa and me.

Still feeling very confident I was cleared of my responsibility, I listened as Michael began to tell me that he was the geologist there at the Guadalupe Mountains. My mind is going, "Big whoopee."

I was shocked; however, at what came next out of Michael's mouth, "My job is to study the wells here in the mountains. I might actually be of assistance to you."

DIGGING A WELL: WHAT STOPS YOUR WELL?

I thought "God, you have got to be kidding me. Seriously! Seriously! Is this really taking place?"

Michael said, "I have an office right over here and if you would like, you can plug your laptop into the power supply. While it is charging, I can answer any questions you might have about the wells in this area."

After plugging the computer in, I excused myself and took off running back to the truck to get Lisa. In total amazement we both went back into Michael's office. We listened intently, gathering gems of information as he spoke.

During the interview, Michael stated that there are many wells in these mountains that no longer have flowing water.

Lisa, being very wise, stopped him at this point and asked, "Why did the streams quit flowing and stop the water supply to the wells?"

He explained that there was an earthquake in the area that shifted the land. As the land shifted, the streams were cut off.

Did you catch that? An earthquake changed the direction of the water flow. Have you been there? No, I'm not talking about the Guadalupe Mountains. Have you ever had an earthquake in your life, a tragedy that changed the direction of the flow in your life from that moment on?

I can almost feel the emotions of some of you readers as you can mark the spot. It's been underlined, bolded, highlighted and, mind you, it is in italics. It jumps right out in your mind. It may have been when one of your parents committed suicide. It could have been when you were raped. It may have been when a loved one was killed, or your newborn was born, only to pass away.

It is easy to identify the earthquakes in our lives because of the immediate effects they have. After that point, we are never the same.

DIGGING A WELL — WHAT STOPS YOUR WELL?

One day you are happy and life is going good. The next day you wake up and there is nothing but fog and gloom.

A trip to the McDonald Observatory, an Astronomy Observation Center close to Ft. Davis, Texas, made me do some thinking. We drove three and a half hours to attend a "Star Party."

Before the Star Party began, the clouds began to move in across the sky. It was time to begin star gazing but there were no stars to be seen. As the moon was shining through the clouds, the star guide discussed some specifics about it.

As we looked, one star began to peek through the clouds. Slowly, two or three more stars began to follow the example of the first. Knowing there were billions of stars in the sky, I began to ponder the situation. Even though there are times when the moon may not be visible to us, we all know that it is there every single night.

Likewise, each of those stars faithfully shines through our every night sky. Saturn, Jupiter, Venus, Neptune, Mercury, and all the other planets are there nightly. However, there we sat under the vast expansion of stars and planets without being able to view the presence of their grandeur.

This is exactly what happens to us when we are inside of the Well of Despair. We look around and blame God for not being there. We blame our friends and family for not being there. There are times when they may abandon us.

Most of the time, those who truly love us will be there for us. God will always be there for us. Yet, through our emotional clouds, we often become unaware of his presence and even convince ourselves that he has gone away.

As humans, none of us are immune. Our problems overwhelm us, cause the clouds to roll in and put a curtain between us and God.

DIGGING A WELL — WHAT STOPS YOUR WELL?

Thinking of the parallel between the human race and the universe, we can see that God is our "Sun." He is our constant. He is the reason that we shine. Our friends and family are a lot like those other stars and planets. They are typically there but throughout time, even a star will burn out. We can hope and pray that our family and friends will stick with us to the end, but sometimes they aren't that reliable because they are human. Most often they are there, but we just can't see them through the clouds. However we know that our God will never burn out.

While visiting the Well of Despair, after great trauma in my own life, the Lord simply laid on my heart these three words: "Walk with me." He didn't say I had to attend church every service, play the piano, sing in the choir or teach a Sunday School class. He just used three words, "Walk with me."

After a few years of being out of the well and on my way to recovery, I was able to sit down and write a song called "The Path." I didn't write it while I was in the well or even six months later. It took years before I was able to write songs of what I experienced.

You may never write a song, paint a picture, or write a book that represents the depth of your pain. Whatever the Lord leads you to do, do it with all your might.

THE PATH

When you are afraid and feel so alone
I will be your Comforter.
When I walked upon the earth
I saw just how it felt to be left all alone.
Kneeling in the garden there

DIGGING A WELL — WHAT STOPS YOUR WELL?

I was left alone to deal with all the pain,
Knowing I was born to die
There upon the cross in just a few short days.
So I turned to God and He gave me peace.

I lifted up my eyes.
I turned my face to God.
He lifted me up and gave me strength to trod
That path.

When you are lost, cannot find your way,
I will be your Counselor.
When you walk upon the earth,
Know within your heart
You will not be left alone.
Kneeling in your sorrow there,
You are not alone to deal with all the pain.
Know that I was born to die
There upon the cross to suffer in your place.
So turn to God; He will give you peace

So lift up your eyes
And turn your face to God.
He will lift you up
And give you strength to trod.
So lift up your eyes
And turn your face to God.
He will lift you up

WHAT STOPS YOUR WELL?

And give you strength to trod
Your path.[11]

The Lord is the only one who can know your sorrow, understand your pain, and touch your soul.

---

[11] Walk With Me and The Path can be downloaded from Amazon.com

DIGGING A WELL — WHAT STOPS YOUR WELL?

The only promise on which to stand,
Is the promise from heaven above.
"I will never leave nor forsake you."
It's in the rainbow of God's love.

CHAPTER SEVEN

"NO WAY!"

Emma, our granddaughter, had just awakened from her nap. Those of us closest to Emma all know what that means!

Emma is just the sweetest, most loving and adorable child that has ever walked upon the face of the earth. However, when she wakes from a nap, I just know that someone had sneaked into her bedroom while our backs were turned. Whoever did this must have traded our Emma for a very upset and frustrated little girl.

You can ask her a question and her answer is never "Yes." Her answer is not "Maybe." She does not even say "No."

You can ask softly and sweetly, but the answer is always the same. "No way!"

DIGGING A WELL — "NO WAY!"

On this particular day, Josh summoned us all to the table. He asked Emma if she wanted to sit on the bench to eat.

"No way!"

Do you want to sit by MeeMee?

"No way!"

Do you want milk?

"No way!"

Would you like a sit with me?

"No way!"

As parents, we all know she will have to eat in order to survive, but at this point she isn't thinking about surviving.

Neither Josh nor Kristy shoves food down her throat, hits her or forces her to eat. They know that in time Emma will wake up enough and decide to eat without being prodded.

Watching Emma go through this process reminded me of a time that the Lord wanted me to be in fellowship with him – to read, teach his word, play the piano, to be a Pastor's wife and to live for him. I was much like little Emma.

When the Lord spoke to me about doing his will, my response was, "No way!" See, I had been hurt and there was no way that I was going to allow myself to be wounded again by people who professed Jesus Christ.

I felt that if I stayed away from the word of God, the house of God, and the people of God, I would be safe.

The Lord continued to ask me to serve him and I continued to say, "No way!" He had to meet me not where I used to be, nor where I would be in five years but he had to meet me exactly where I was at that moment.

When Emma wakes from her nap, she just wants her Mommy to hold her. Emma needs to be held until she feels secure with everything and everyone.

DIGGING A WELL
"NO WAY!"

Once Emma has the feeling of security, she will gladly cooperate. However, without this security there is no cooperation from Miss Emma.

One day I remembered my heavenly Father saying, "Walk with me." My response was, "No way!"

I said, "I don't think I'm ready."

My Father said, "I'm not going to make you teach. I'm not going to make you sing. I'm not going to make you play the piano, or even be a helper. Just walk with me."

As I heard the gentle wooing of my Father, I finally agreed that I would walk with him. All he wanted to do was feed my soul. As I opened the word of God, he gently led me to attend church once again. He was giving me the assurance that I wouldn't have to have deep interaction.

I attended church for approximately six months and always sat on the back row. Slowly I began to wake up, realizing that I was getting more involved in the church. I was no longer pushing him away, saying, "No way!"

The Lord has walked with me slowly, never pushing, never demanding – just walking with me.

So here I am, back in the ministry, playing the piano, speaking to women about deep pain and witnessing to them as they develop a closer walk with the Lord.

Never would I walk out of Emma's life just because she said, "No way!" I know what a precious spirit she is to Christ.

This is what your Father sees in you. He sees you as pure and clean and filled with his love. He is longing for you to fully wake up, so that he can see you laugh, dance, and bless other people's lives.

God is willing to wait patiently until you are ready. He will not push or demand, and most of all, he will not leave you. He is waiting with tender eyes of love and open arms the moment you are ready to return to him.

Once you wake up to whispers of fear, doubt, and frustration. God is waiting to hear you say to Satan. "NO WAY!"

This is one of the songs I wrote after I came out of the Well of Despair realizing the Lord would be with me each step of the way. This song was written about these three words the Lord spoke to me: "Walk with me." It truly expresses how I was feeling. I knew that I would never make it on my own, so this became my prayer.

Walk with Me

Lord I'll follow you.
I will walk with you.
I will go where you lead me.
Father, be my guide,
Walking by my side.
You said you'll never leave me.
Walk with me. Talk to me.

I'll go where you lead.
Give me what I need.
Walk with me.
Talk to me.

I'll go where you lead.
Give me what I need.

| DIGGING A WELL | "NO WAY!" |

Walk with me.
Talk to me.

Savior, like a Shepherd, lead us.
Much we need thy tender care.
In thy pleasant pastures feed us.
For our use thy folds prepare,
Walk with me.
Talk with me.

I'll go where you lead.
Give me what I need.
Walk with me.
Talk to me.

Thou hast promised to receive us,
Poor and sinful though we be.
Thou hast mercy to relieve us,
Grace to cleanse and power to free.

Walk with me.
Talk to me.
I'll go where you lead.
Give me what I need.
Walk with me.
Talk to me.

Lord I'll follow you.

I will walk with you.
I will go where you lead me.
Father, be my guide,
Walking by my side,
You said you'll never leave me.

Blessed Jesus, Blessed Jesus,
Thou hast bought us, thine we are.
Blessed Jesus, Blessed Jesus,
Thou hast bought us, thine we are.
You said you'll never leave me alone.[12]

---

[12] My sister, Kay Rowe, helped me complete this song. As I was writing and had a mental block, Kay came along and helped me get the words flowing once again.

CHAPTER EIGHT

RIVER OF LIFE

*Now there was set a
vessel full of vinegar:
and they filled a
spunge with vinegar,
and put it upon hyssop,
and put it to his mouth.
When Jesus therefore
had received the vinegar,
he said,
"It is finished"
and he bowed his head,*

and gave up the ghost.
John 19:29-30

Do you realize that during the crucifixion the soldiers offered Jesus a vessel full of vinegar? We see Jesus drinking from the bitter cup. Satan thought he was victorious at this point.

We can look at drinking from the vessel of bitterness in a symbolic sense as well. When we drink from the cup of bitterness, Satan rejoices. He realizes he has gotten a grip on our lives.

When Jesus received the vinegar, he said, "It is finished."

This is what I imagine may have taken place when Satan heard those words. The taunting began. Satan said, "I heard you myself when you said, 'It is finished.' Everyone knows what 'It is finished' means. I saw you as you bowed your head and took your last breath! I watched as they wrapped your dead body in the burial cloth!"

Jesus bowed his head, and gave up the ghost. All the angels in heaven watched as Satan and his demons began to do the whoop whoop dance. I can envision him now saying, "Oh yeah! Oh yeah! Jesus the Messiah, he is dead! Oh yeah! Oh yeah! Jesus the Messiah, he is dead!"

Satan is now thinking, "They just put the body inside the tomb and placed a huge bolder over the entrance.

I'm beginning to smell the smell of victory."

"He said he was going to save the world, yet he couldn't even save himself.

Did I not hear you tell the woman at the well... now, just what was it you said? Oh yeah... I think you said you were the Living Water, and that she would never thirst again.

Well, what do you say now Jesus?"

> *The Jews therefore,*
> *because it was the preparation,*
> *that the bodies should not remain*
> *upon the cross on the Sabbath day,*
> *(for that Sabbath day was a high day,)*
> *besought Pilate that their*
> *legs might be broken,*
> *and that they might be taken away.*
> *Then came the soldiers,*
> *and brake the legs of the first,*
> *and of the other which*
> *was crucified with him.*
> *But when they came to Jesus,*
> *and saw that he was dead already,*
> *they brake not his legs:*
> *But one of the soldiers with a spear*
> *pierced his side, and forthwith came*
> *there out blood and water.*
> *John 19:30-33*

Look closely at what took place at this moment. Even Satan himself, as wise and powerful as he thought he was, did not see what took place. When the spear was thrust into Jesus' side, it no longer mattered that the well flowed where he had met the woman. As we see wells are no longer mentioned in the scripture.

This was the earthquake of all earthquakes. As we reflect

DIGGING A WELL
RIVER OF LIFE

back on chapter six, we are reminded what an earthquake can do to the flow of a well.

This event, the crucifixion of Christ, changed the course of history.

From that moment, that very instant, the world changed. The sun turned dark. As the earth shook, the thick veil of the temple was torn from top to bottom. After this event, even the calendars changed. Nothing was left the same.

Our scripture states, "forthwith came there out blood and water." Christ himself said that we no longer need Jacob's well because we have a "well of water springing up into everlasting life."

> There is a fountain filled with blood,
> Drawn from Immanuel's veins
> And sinners plunged beneath that flood
> Lose all their guilty stains.
> Lose all their guilty stains.
> Lose all their guilty stains.
> And sinners plunged beneath that flood
> Lose all their guilty stains
> E'er since, by faith, I saw the stream.
> Thy flowing wounds supply.
> Redeeming love has been my theme,
> And shall be till I die.
> And shall be till I die,
> And shall be till I die
> Redeeming love has been my theme,
> And shall be till I die[13]

---

[13] There is a fountain, written by William Cowpen-Public Domain

DIGGING A WELL — RIVER OF LIFE

After Jesus' crucifixion, wells are never again mentioned again in the scripture. We now have the River of Life that flows straight from the throne of God.

> *And he shewed me a pure*
> *river of water of life, clear as crystal,*
> *proceeding out of the*
> *throne of God and of the Lamb.*
> *Revelation 22:1*

Can you imagine Satan and his angels looking on as the stone was rolled away? Jesus walked out of that tomb. He had all the power and authority to tear Satan apart but God's ways are not our ways.

Christ chose to show himself to a select few. He led them to spread the news of his resurrection so that more people would have the opportunity to drink from the Living Water. He wants us all to drink from the water that flows from his wounded side.

> *But whosoever drinketh of the water*
> *that I shall give him shall never thirst;*
> *but the water that I shall give him*
> *shall be in him a well of water*
> *springing up into everlasting life.*
> *John 4:14*

> *In the midst of the street of it,*
> *and on either side of the river,*
> *was there the tree of life,*

DIGGING A WELL — RIVER OF LIFE

> *which bare twelve manner of fruits,*
> *and yielded her fruit every month:*
> *and the leaves of the tree were*
> *for the healing of the nations.*
> *Revelation 22:2*

In order to be able to drink from the living water, we will need to empty our hearts and minds of worldly things. We must come to him as empty vessels before being filled with his Spirit.

The love Christ will put in our empty vessels will become an overflowing and all consuming well.

> *Then cometh he to a city*
> *of Samaria which is called Sychar,*
> *near to the parcel of ground*
> *that Jacob gave to his son Joseph.*
> *Now Jacob's well was there.*
> *Jesus therefore,*
> *being wearied with his journey,*
> *sat thus on the well:*
> *and it was about the sixth hour.*
> *There cometh a woman*
> *of Samaria to draw water:*
> *Jesus saith unto her,*
> *"Give me to drink."*
> *John 4:5-7*

We see Jesus sitting at a well that Jacob dug hundreds of

years before. When Jacob was traveling through the land, do you think he ever thought that the Messiah himself would someday drink from his well? Yet, here he is. He offered the Samaritan woman a drink. He asked her to drink "the Living Water" which only he could give.

On Wednesdays, in our church, we would usually had about fifteen to twenty kids at church. It seemed as if overnight that we doubled. The next week we doubled again. What was taking place in Kermit, Texas? We were sharing "the Living Water."

The children attending our church began to see things in a new light. They invited their friends, who invited their friends, and within a short amount of time we were running over a hundred students on Wednesdays.

These students aren't just coming once in a while, they are attending faithfully. God has allowed us to witness many of these children come to the saving knowledge of the Lord Jesus Christ.

Determined that every child coming through the doors of our church would receive a Bible, I began to pray. Driving to Odessa one day my father called and asked me how things were going. I shared with him the desire, deep within the well of my heart – placing a Bible in the hands of every child that walks through the church doors.

My father, who lives in Tennessee, called a publisher. Just like that, there were one hundred seventy-five Bibles sent to be distributed to the children of Kermit.

Dad, living so far away, may not be here to physically see what's happening. However, I believe that God will allow him to see his works upon entering the gates of heaven.

The following article appeared in the Kermit Newspaper not too long after we started giving the Bibles away. It appears to be several articles but it was written as one.

"Miracle on Mulberry Street"

Two waves have pounded ashore in this decade:

> The first of these two shouted:

YOUTH ARE JUMPING SHIP, ABANDONING CHURCH ACTIVITIES...... SHIPS' CAPTAINS REPORT STEADY LOSS OF YOUTH; AT THIS RATE A WHOLE GENERATION IS UNACCOUNTED FOR.

"More recently voices have been raised to question this pessimistic view:

> This second wave reports:

MORE POSITIVE PARTICIPATION BY YOUTH. WITNESSES HAVE STEPPED UP TO VOUCH FOR A MORE DYNAMIC, HEALTHY ROBUST CHURCH IN OUR TIMES THAN BELIEVED. They point to huge numbers of new believers in China, Central and South America, sub Saharan Africa and Pacific Islands.

A good number of evangelicals believe that the voices of doom and gloom have misled us by their insistence that the church (including youth) is dying. Predictably, like Peter, we believe "what we have seen and heard." see Acts 4:19.

If you visit the Northside Baptist Church, Kermit, on a Wednesday evening you will see and hear Kermit's youth in a mighty manifestation of the Lord who is very much alive.

In season and out of season the congregation's youth ministry draws scores of youth. They range from elementary to high school age. For the school year, attendance tops a cool 102 to 105 most every Wednesday. Summer numbers more typically reach around 75.

May I call it "THE MIRACLE ON MULBERRY STREET?"

Hot and hearty suppers served by head chef Becky Boss and her fellow "deacons" are unquestionably a grand attraction. What happens when all have feasted? To a man (or woman) the kids clean up their spot. They carry trash to a can. Then each youth carries their chairs to get them out of the way.

It may not look just like that the night you visit. For example a large bunch of teens sit in pews for their after-supper activity. (I'm not saying that they come carrying a pew like a chair). Although, the feeling you get is this: There are so many well behaved, cheerful but not loud, not crazy kids; rather polite, friendly, respectful, good humored, really cool folk who have either embraced Jesus Christ or may be close to it. I believe that if there were good reason to do so, these kids could carry pews wherever they were needed.

BULLETIN: Four Northside adults recently took 50 kids to the rodeo.

After supper, everybody goes to their room for an hour of Bible study, discussion, drama, singing, a movie and discussion. These adults take the lead. You may know what super people they are: Andy and Lana Williamson, Levis Awbrey, Sherry Long, Charles and Angie Litchford, Sarina Rogers and Joni Taylor. The pastor, Steve Long, hopes we haven't left any names out. I know how he feels and I accept the responsibility.

Steve sets up the tables on Wednesday mornings. James Cotton directs recreation before the meal. Weldon & Wannah Hartley, Melvin Boss, Karen Fischer, Janet Sledge, and Rose Stewart serve regularly on Becky's kitchen crew. Others pitch in from time to time as needed. Bobbie Dale Cotton plays the piano.

These are the same servants of Jesus Christ who choose to open up an hour earlier to accommodate kids who appreciate supervised outdoor recreation. Members held a money raiser to gain cash for recreation equipment.

My neighbor, Levis Awbrey brought my attention to Northside. He and his two sons are right in there on Wednesday nights. As Levis says: "The kids could eat our great meals and just leave afterwards.... They choose to stay.

Late Breaking News;

Some days after this column was written, I received the awesome news that 63 young men and woman reported to Andy Williamson's teenage class on Wednesday Feb 1, 2012. Andy is assisted by Levis Awbrey.

Sixty-three were recorded in contrast to the more frequent count of fifty-three.

In retrospect this news confirms the relationship between periods of intensive prayer and spiritual awakening. Whether an earlier fifty-three or the latest sixty-three we can only praise our true God to whom belongs these mighty works. Pastors in their weekly prayer hour had voiced to the Lord over a two-year period their earnest pleas for a spiritual awakening in Winkler County.

Article by Rod Peacock[14]

Being the pastor's wife of this church, I can tell you that there have been several "Miracles on Mulberry Street." We have seen God move in a powerful way. There have been times that I felt there was an angel on the top of our church that beckoned the children as the scripture says.

> *"But Jesus said, Suffer little children,*
> *and forbid them not, to come unto me:*
> *for of such is the kingdom of heaven."*
> *Matthew 19:14*

Do we get discouraged at times? Of course we do! Do we send out a plea for more workers to help us? By all means, yes! Do we know where to turn to when we need help? Yes!

> *"Jesus answered and said unto her,*
> *Whosoever drinketh of this*
> *water shall thirst again:*
> *But whosoever drinketh of the water*
> *that I shall give him shall never thirst;*
> *but the water that I shall give him*

---

[14] Winkler County News, Kermit Texas

DIGGING A WELL — RIVER OF LIFE

shall be in him a well of water
springing up into everlasting life.
John 4:13-14

He also says he owns the cattle on a thousand hills and that his wealth is unlimited. Many times we have prayed and reminded the Lord that these are his children. Since he owns the cattle on a thousand hills, we really need him to sell one. We need him to provide the money for us to feed all these hungry little mouths.

We have earnestly prayed for workers of the harvest. We are seeing the Lord answer those prayers. Recently, we have been blessed by a number of families joining and stepping in to help us.

We are in constant need of God's care. Daily we turn to him as our Great Comforter. He is teaching us, step by step, how to dig a Well of Salvation right here where we live.

Once our people saw a glimpse of the Well of Beer-lahairoi, meaning the power and vision of God, and were willing to let others come into the church and drink from the Well of Salvation, things began to change.

We started passing out Bibles to every child that walked through the church doors. Immediately we began to see the Well of Rehoboth, meaning fruitfulness or enlarging.

Northside came to a standstill one Wednesday night. The discussion was on whether or not to allow the rowdy community children to continue to attend services. God intervened. It was settled. The body came together and stood upon the word of God. We united as a church and began to offer the Well of Salvation to those children.

Northside would not be experiencing the Well of Rehoboth

DIGGING A WELL — RIVER OF LIFE

or the Well of Beer-lahairoi today if we had not listened and obeyed the Lord's command.

Had our decision not been to dig a well, we would have lost our testimony to these children, as well as to the community. Since God's intervention, there have been times that I didn't know if we could handle the blessings that he bestowed upon us.

Come! Drink from the Well of Salvation with us. Experience the great things the Lord is doing.

You may feel as I did before speaking at one of my Ladies' Teas. Preparing for this Ladies' Tea, I felt like the woman that had visited Jesus at the well – empty, with nothing to give. How could I serve him with this emptiness inside?

"What are you filled with?" This question came to me one morning, driving to work. I began to think about the Ladies' Tea that I should be preparing for. Expressing to the Lord this emptiness that needed filling, I was not a little empty; I was bone dry empty! I had nothing to give the ladies. Never before, when planning a ladies meeting, had I found myself in this state.

The Lord usually gives me three-fourths of what I am to speak on. Sometimes when he waits until the last moment to reveal the closing of the subject, this is quite scary for me. I am the type of person that needs to see the whole picture. But this time, I was seeing nothing.

As I was driving down a lonely road between Kermit and Andrews, Texas, the Lord began to show me exactly why he brought me to this point. The words to the song "Empty I Come to You" began to flow from my mouth. The feeling of astonishment came over me as I realized that the Ladies' Tea was to be on the theme, Why the Lord wants us to be empty.

EMPTY I COME TO YOU

Empty, I come to you;
I want to see your face.
Empty, I come to you;
Come fill this holy place.
I want to see your power.
I want to see your strength.
Fill me with your mercy;
Come, fill me with your peace.
Empty, I come to you;
Come fill me with your grace.

Empty, we come to you;
We want to see your face.
Empty, we come to you;
Come fill this holy place.
We want to see your power.
We want to feel your strength.
Fill us with your mercy;
Lord, fill us with your peace.
Empty, we come to you;
Come fill us with your grace.

| DIGGING A WELL | LEAVE MY CHILDREN ALONE! |

CHAPTER NINE

LEAVE MY CHILDREN ALONE!

Have you ever wanted to hurt someone badly? It doesn't take most of us very long to get upset when someone wrongs us.

If someone does something harmful to one of your children, the reaction is many times stronger. If you see something happen to your child your muscles tense up, the heart rate increases and your adrenaline kicks in.

If it happens again, the reaction is much stronger. After repeated times, every muscle in your body reacts, and woe to the person that keeps hurting your child.

I remember back when my sister and I attended school in San Antonio, Texas. We walked about ten or twelve blocks to

DIGGING A WELL
LEAVE MY CHILDREN ALONE!

school every day. Many of the kids in San Antonio were pretty rough, very rough.

One day, walking home from school, a gang circled one of the boys walking just a few paces in front of us. Everyone stopped in their tracks. As they began to beat him, nobody moved. They were beating him to a bloody pulp and none of us stepped in to save the boy for fear we would be their next victim.

A little old lady came out of her apartment about the time one of the boys pulled a knife and started cutting Frank's face. She was feeble. Nevertheless she walked over there and began to smack those boys with her cane. She told them to get out of her neighborhood and never come back. The gang could hear the sirens in the distance and took off running.

Frank was not her child but the little old lady intervened on his behalf. She was angry and her anger caused her to step up to the plate and chase the boys away.

When God created the angelic beings he never said, "this is my child." I never saw in the scripture where it stated that he breathed into them the breath of life. He never states that he walked with them in the garden or desired them to be like him.

When Satan began to think he could be greater than God, he led some angels away from glorifying God. He wanted to be above God. Many people have asked this question, "Why did God kick Satan and his angels out of heaven and do nothing more? Why didn't he destroy them right then and there?"

God loves his children more than life itself. He gave his Son as a sacrifice for us. Our Father loved the angels but he loved mankind even more.

Christ loved us enough to lay down his life. When Lucifer did wrong, Christ didn't lay down his life for him. This puts mankind and Satan on different levels.

LEAVE MY CHILDREN ALONE!

After God created the sun, moon, stars, and all the wonders of the earth, he saw that creation was still incomplete. On the sixth day, he created mankind.

*And God said,
Let us make man in our image,
after our likeness:
and let them have dominion
over the fish of the sea,
and over the fowl of the air,
and over the cattle,
and over all the earth,
and over every creeping thing
that creepeth upon the earth.
So God created man
in his own image,
in the image of God
created he him;
male and female created he them.
Genesis 1:26-27*

It also says God breathed into man his breath. That breath gave him life. In 1 John 3:1 and many other places, we are called the sons of God.

Woven all through the scripture it's the concept that we are his children if we believe and follow him.

One of the reasons God's wrath toward Satan is so strong is because of God's love and protection toward his children.

The wrath of a father or mother is much stronger if an

DIGGING A WELL
LEAVE MY CHILDREN ALONE!

enemy directs his hostility toward their child.

Let's move our attention back to Frank in San Antonio. He was about to get his eyes cut out with a knife from a boy called Fat Albert. This boy was very intimidating, and there were some other boys that followed and looked up to him. They were the "Fat Albert Gang." All the kids knew to stay clear of Fat Albert and his gang.

After beating Frank, Fat Albert's life changed. Little did Fat Albert know he had messed with the wrong person!

Frank's father was ticked off and said that he was going to kill the boy! "Don't know when, don't know where, and don't know how, but that boy is going down." The word began to circulate around the school, "Don't be caught with Fat Albert"

When Satan pulled the angels away and persuaded them to follow him instead of God, this angered God. But when he began to do the same with God's children, we see all throughout scripture just how angry God became.

In Revelation, we read the rest of the story – the destruction of Satan. It will not be a pretty sight. I don't claim to understand all of what the book of Revelation says, but I do know that I am the Lord's child and he is coming after Satan. I don't know when, but I do know where and how – Satan is going down.

The Lord will do the same with Satan as Frank's father did with Fat Albert. Hundreds of years ago, a book was written that sent out a warning to all those who might want to hang out with Satan. The scripture pronounces woe to them. The word has been spread all over the world. He is waiting for the perfect moment.

Just as Frank's father sent out a message, the Lord is asking you to tell your friends and for them to tell their friends, that the day is coming. When it does, woe to Satan and his gang.

Fat Albert did come up missing. As far as I know he was never found.

Just as Frank's father sent out the warning, the Lord said he is sick and tired of his children being pushed around, tempted and lied to, tempting them to do evil.

One day he will say, "Today is the day!" Christ will come, riding on a white horse, leading his army. For all the times you have been wronged, he will unleash his fury upon Satan and his gang in one great swift moment. The Lord will come and enforce what he's said:

"LEAVE MY CHILDREN ALONE!"

The Lord has saved that moment for himself. He is coming as our judge. Some people will be sitting at a game, others shopping, some reading a book. He will say one day, "It is time." When Jesus comes back riding on a white horse in all his majesty, Satan is going to try to run and hide.

For all the times the Lord said, "Judge not lest ye be judged," for the times he has said, "Turn the other cheek," for all the times you were left hurting and suffering because of the horrible things that happened in life, he is going to say, "My child, I have come to judge those who have harmed you."

Woe to anyone who has wounded one of my precious children. Woe to you that cursed and mocked my children. Woe to Satan, the prince and the power of the air and to his angels who have caused earthquakes in people's lives. My Father has prepared an eternal place for you called hell where there is weeping and gnashing of teeth. This is a place where your thirst can never be quenched throughout eternity. You can no longer destroy lives, cause pain or touch one of my children." You will never be able to walk or crawl out of it.

That's my Father who is coming to do more than just kick you out of heaven, Satan. My Father is the Lord God Almighty. He is the Great Judge. He is the Alpha and the Omega. He is the Beginning and the End. He is my All in All and he will have the final say!

A REAL EYE OPENER

Preparing for the possibility of having neck surgery, I woke up from having a discogram on May 13th of this year.

Nothing could have prepared me for this procedure. I read articles, forums, watched videos, and everything I could get my hands on in order to know everything possible about the procedure.

Lying on the bed, getting ready to go back for the procedure, a nice calm nurse came in to check on me and try to settle any anxiety before the procedure. She kindly said, "Anything you have read about this procedure, throw out the window. At this clinic we do things a bit differently."

Ah, relaxation! Little did I know the relaxation was only temporary. Things were going to change.

Nothing I read said what followed the procedure was an experience worse than the actual surgery itself. My advice to anyone needing this procedure is run! Hide! Hide under the largest rock you can find. Change doctors and tell the next doctor that you've already had a discogram. Do anything in the world to keep from having this procedure!

The moment I woke up from the discogram, I realized why it was required for me to have it. While I thought it was to find out what discs needed replacing, actually it was God's will for me to have this experience so I could learn something new.

Right before being given the anesthetic a nurse gave me a

shot into my IV. The nurse said, "We are giving you this shot to dry your saliva."

Honestly, if you have ever had this shot you will know that what she said was an understatement.

The first thought I had when waking up was, "Oh my, I just can't imagine what hell is like," because hell is a place where thirst is never quenched.

The nurse came in to check on me. I said, "I need a drink."

She kindly looked at me with her brown eyes and patted my arm and said, "Honey, I know you are thirsty but we just can't give you anything."

I am normally a patient person but right then I was about to come off that bed! That was, until I rose up and began to feel the pain in my neck. After several minutes of pleading with the nurse she brought me a piece of ice.

"Honestly! One little piece of ice. I'm literally going to die of thirst lying here in the hospital with nurses all around me!" I thought.

About ten minutes later, the nurse came back in with some more ice and said,

"Honey, be sure and suck on the ice slowly so that you don't get nauseated."

I didn't care at that point if I lost my stomach. I thought, "Just give me the cup of ice and get out of my room."

Later, my nurse returned with a big smile and said, "I have a can of apple juice for you."

I kindly looked back at her and said, "Just one little can of juice? I'm positive that one can of apple juice isn't sufficient for what I'm experiencing."

She assured me that as soon as I finished the bottle of apple juice, she would bring me another one. By the time I finished the second bottle of apple juice it was time to be released. I was getting dressed and asked the nurse for more to drink.

Steve said he would stop and get me a drink at a convenience store on the way home. I assured him that the convenience store was not quite close enough.

My nurse was one of those who showed great compassion for her patients and gave me a can of apple juice to go. Bless her heart. If the pain weren't so great, I would have jumped up and given her a hug.

The first night after the procedure, at my son's house in Garland, Texas I experienced a significant amount of pain. I couldn't turn my head, or rise up. I needed water every ten minutes. I had received a really large cup that had a scripture on it from a lady at our church. I finally tucked the cup in the crease of my arm, packed pillows all around it and put my straw where I could slightly tilt my head every ten minutes and take a sip of water.

Five weeks after the discogram, I had an artificial disc replacement and a two-level fusion in my neck. What I experienced during the discogram was much worse than my actual surgery. It took me about twelve days to recover from the discogram.

To this day I don't go anywhere without a glass or bottle of water. I am a changed woman. I never again want to experience the dry, parched feeling that I experienced that day.

If I weren't a born again Christian before that procedure, I promise you I would have been after that day.

My desire is that every person that reads this book will be able to stop at the Well of Salvation, be led to the Living Water and experience the abundant life that Christ gives freely.

CHAPTER TEN

GREATEST LOVER OF ALL TIMES

Now that headline would catch the attention of any male or female walking through the checkout line. Curiosity, beyond measure, would be spinning out of control. This article is better than any written in Sports Illustrated and has a picture that makes the mind run in every direction. Anyone covered by Seventeen magazines has never even come close to touching the surface of this lover. It's a wonder we haven't seen this on all the tabloids in America.

I can see it now – people lining up for hours to see this lover. They want to get a smell of the fragrance of this lover, to get close enough to touch, or get a close-up picture. Oh, to savor the moment of the time spent together!

GREATEST LOVER OF ALL TIMES

Imagine a lover that fears nothing, and will never break your heart. There's a beauty that is beyond explanation. Self praise is given but not in arrogance.

Our society teaches that love is won by outward beauty but as we gaze upon this lover, we know otherwise.

Magnificent beauty!
Glorious beauty!
Awesome beauty!

Is this not what we search for? Are we not all looking for that person at one time or another? Whether male or female we all long for this type of relationship. We long to be cherished, lavished upon, doted over and honored.

We desire a lover that is not just willing to give five minutes out of the day, but willing to spend the whole day together. You may be wondering, just who is this lover?

"Your fragrance is unexplainable. One slight breath can relax all of one's senses – take one's anxiety away. The aroma of your presence sweeps one away into a place of relaxation, peace and comfort!

Your appearance, so pure, and your beauty send a message to everyone.

I am the one, yes; I am the one that you need! I am not arrogant but I am confident that I can be your all in all. I can meet your every need. I bring satisfaction to your soul.

Your soul is satisfied, and when you find this satisfaction immediately it brings your mind and heart to follow.

Your taste is sweet, relaxing every muscle, as never before. Nerves are calmed and strength is gained.

My soul is at peace in your presence.

You are never indecent and your excellence is exceedingly great. You are free of suspicion, of vanity, yet you give yourself for all."

> *"I Am the Rose of Sharon,*
> *the lily of the field"*
> *Solomon 2:1*

This poetry of love was written by Solomon but is also a picture of Christ. He is wooing you. He is enticing you, lifting and praising you. He is in love with you. Not in an indecent way but in a pure, righteous way.

The Rose of Sharon can be eaten and is sweet to the taste. Hummingbirds are drawn to this flower, for its nectar is among the sweetest of all flowers.

It is drank as herbal tea and used for medicinal purposes for the following ailments: Bronchitis, respiratory infections, urinary tract infections, wrinkles. It is used for antivirus, antibacterial medicine, reduction of inflammation and anti-hemorrhaging. It strengthens the immune system. It quiets the nerves and elevates emotions.

The Rose of Sharon is used as oil for massages. It is said to heal one's wounds faster than normal. It is also used for incense to calm one's spirits.

There are actually many flowers that are called Rose of Sharon. The first one I saw was solid white with a crimson red center. With this picture before my eyes, I understood why the Lord Jesus Christ has been referred to for many centuries as the "Rose of Sharon."

The blood red that is in the center of the flower reminded me of a carnation that had been sitting in red food coloring.

Symbolically speaking, when we allow the blood of Jesus to flow through our veins, there will be evidence of it in our lives. Our sins will be made white as snow.

This flower has both male and female reproductive units; therefore, it is called "The perfect flower." This leads us to the conclusion that whether male or female, you are welcome to come into his presence.

> *There is neither Jew nor Greek,*
> *there is neither bond nor free,*
> *there is neither male nor female:*
> *for ye are all one in Christ Jesus.*
> *Galatians 3:28*

When Solomon wrote about the Rose of Sharon, he may have been reflecting on a valley in that area where his bride lived called "Sharon Valley." There were actually two different valleys with this name in Israel.

One valley was a very large valley and the other one was a smaller valley. This signifies that there is room for everyone in his presence.

The seeds on the Rose of Sharon are numerous. We need to be out planting those seeds so we can see a harvest of souls in our nation and in our world.

The flower itself is in the shape of a trumpet, suggesting the need to herald the message out.

> *"Christ is the fullness of him*
> *that filleth all in all.*
> *Ephesians 1:23*

Another way of saying this is: "He is Christ, The Rose of Sharon."

Let's face it; we live in a very sensual day and age. We have commercials, movies and magazines that promote this sensuality constantly.

America is on a downhill slide. One can't shop in the grocery store without having tabloids enticing them in. Just fifteen minutes in front of the television should give us an idea how sensual we have become. Advertisers have learned to exhibit sexuality to sell their products.

The Lord formed us with these kinds of desires but he did it for his glory, not our own. The need is to know the depth of the "Rose of Sharon," there are thousands of men and women in our nation that are longing to fill a place in their hearts. They are reaching for all the items that only give temporary fulfillment, instead of fulfillment that satisfies the soul.

The final truth I would like for you to see about the Rose of Sharon is this: Humans can safely taste and eat of it. Sheep can – even cows. All creatures can eat this lovely plant except for one. The one living thing it is poison to is a dog.[15]

We love dogs, especially if it's been a family dog, but in the scripture, a dog represents someone less than human. It refers to someone who is evil – someone who is out to destroy your body, mind and soul.

Beware of dogs,
beware of evil workers.
Philippians 3:2

---

[15] The Rose of Sharon-http://wrytestuff.com/swa481007.htm   Sermons by C.H. Spurgeon-http://www.biblebb.com/files/spurgeon/0784.htm
Much of this information was gained as a child listening to my father William Royce Creekmore preach.

Satan is out to destroy us. He doesn't want us to be victorious, but God's word is our weapon.

> *... the word of God is quick,*
> *and powerful, and sharper than*
> *any two edged sword, piercing*
> *even to the dividing asunder of soul*
> *and spirit, and of the*
> *joints and marrow,*
> *and is a discerner of the thoughts*
> *and intents of the heart.*
> *Hebrews 4:12*

Numerous ladies have told me that they walked out of their marriage because their husband was having an affair or deeply involved in pornography. Brokenhearted and needing this deep love, some turned to another man to fill the void. Others went to male strip bars, trying to make their mate hurt as much as they had been hurt.

We have a nation that is more often seeking the pleasures of this world in place of the pleasures of the Lord. Homes are being destroyed, young people are becoming sexually involved and lives are being torn apart.

There are many of you reading this book right now that are in the Well of Destruction and you don't know how to get out. You can smell the drafty, mucky odor and you hate being this far down in the well. You are engulfed with darkness and there is only one way out.

You want out but you are so afraid that if you begin to move toward the light you might find yourself out in the open with no protection.

You prefer to stay in the well just because it brings you security. You have been there so long it has become your way of life.

Jesus Christ wants to be your "Rose of Sharon." He wants to be your hedge of protection. He wants to satisfy your taste, calm your nerves, and give you rest. You must first take and eat. In other words, you must allow the Lord to have the freedom to do these things in your life.

This is a process. You did not get in this well overnight and you probably will not get out overnight. Don't expect for it to be an immediate fix. Remember you will be climbing out of the Well of Destruction and despair, not jogging. Turn to the Lord and ask him to give you the courage to take baby steps towards recovery.

Just as the doctor does not put salve on a deep wound expecting you will be totally healed the next day, neither does the Lord Jesus Christ. He is a patient God and will walk with you! He is our Jehovah Rapha – "The LORD that healeth thee."[16]

You might say, "I'm not sick. Why did you say 'recovery'? You may not be sick, my friend, but you have been broken.

You may be in the Well of Destruction due to a death in your family. This could be the death of one of your children, maybe an infant. It could be a mother, father, or grandparent. You may have a loved one that took their own life. One thing is certain, you did not ask to go to this well and drink.

One day you just woke up and that is where you found yourself. You may have been raped or nearly murdered and you have no idea how to even start the process of getting out of the well.

---

[16] Exodus 15:26

DIGGING A WELL — GREATEST LOVER OF ALL TIMES

My friend, the first step is to reach your hand out to the "Rose of Sharon". He has never refused anyone.[17] His love is endless. Be willing to open your soul to him. If you open your soul to the "Rose of Sharon," the Lord Jesus Christ, your heart and mind will surely follow.

Once you have opened your soul to him, find a Bible and read Psalms and Proverbs. In these two books you will discover a balm of healing for your soul.

Find a Christian radio station that plays music that will feed your soul, heart and mind. You may not be ready for deep spiritual truths but you will need a diet of love, grace and compassion. You will need to enter into a daily walk with the Lord in order to recover.

In time, as you begin to walk each day, you will see the light at the top of the well.

*You will probably be able to mark
the day the clouds rolled away.*

Sometimes, however, this light brings the fear of being exposed. Don't be afraid, for when you are out in the open, "The Rose of Sharon" will be your hedge of protection.

Many people in the area of the Valley of Sharon would actually plant this magnificent flower as a hedge around their house. We need to surround our lives with Jesus Christ, "The Rose of Sharon."

I know you may see yourself as in a deep, dark, mucky well, but can you visualize yourself in this protective hedge? Get an image in your mind of "The Rose of Sharon" being your hedge of protection. He will surround you with love, comfort,

---

[17] John 6:37

peace and security and will be your defender.

This process may take a month. It may take two. For some of you, it could take several months. The solution requires never going backwards, always looking to the top of the well, each day finding you are one step closer to being out in the sunshine.

There is nothing wrong with you if you are sitting in this well. I assure you that every human that lived or will ever live will find themselves at the brink of this well at one point in time.

The key is, don't stay there.
Find your way out.

Trying to deal with your problems alone may be difficult. You may need to confide in a pastor or counselor. Some may need to see a doctor for assistance.

Don't let Satan push you back down. Keep your eyes on your beautiful Rose of Sharon, the greatest lover of all time!

DIGGING A WELL | GETTING READY FOR THE TRIP

As the snow caps the tops of the mountains
So may the peace of God fall down on you
May it rest there and be visible to others
To the point they know your
life has been touched
by the Creator of the universe.

DIGGING A WELL | GETTING READY FOR THE TRIP

CHAPTER ELEVEN

GETTING READY FOR THE TRIP

So, you're ready to pack your bags and go on this trip with me.

If your child were going on a long trip, a difficult journey, would you let him out of the house without checking his bags? I know, as a mother, there is no way I would have allowed that.

Our heavenly Father is the same way. About a year ago I discovered that I was not properly equipped for the adventure of writing this book. The Lord showed me this in an extremely unusual way.

A Pipeline to the Lost World

As I began to pray about the "Digging a Well" ministry I

ran across a calendar in my office. As it appeared to be several years old and worn, I wondered where it came from. I started to throw it away – then something caught my eye. Opening it up, at the bottom of the page, there was a load of information about equipment used in a pipeline.

As I read all the items required for a pipeline to hold up and run properly, I read that these were the very things that we need to be a pipeline to the lost world.

I'm going to list them in the same order that was listed at the bottom of the calendar and then give my definition to each one. My interpretations are in parentheses.

> Pipe Supports – (Prayer Warriors) – Those who stand and support us in what God is doing.

> Slide Bearings – (Being Flexible) – Our willingness to move in whatever direction that God wants to take us in the ministry.

> Expansion Joints – (Willingness to Grow) –Our readiness to grow and expand into new areas of life and ministry and go places never gone before?

> Insulated Pipe Supports – (Stronger Prayer Warriors) – Not just any prayer warriors but some that are rooted and grounded in the word of God.

> Anchor Bolts – (Word of God) – Being grounded and anchored in the scripture.

> Hold Downs – (Stabilizer) –Someone to hold us

down and keep us from moving in the wrong direction.

> Pressure Vessel – Jesus Christ – (There are qualifications for a pressure vessel.)

1) Subject to the provisions of sub regulation, no user shall use, require or permit the use of any vessel under pressure unless:

> A) It has be designed and constructed in accordance with a health and safety standard incorporated into these regulations. (Jesus Christ meets up to all of God's highest standards)[18]

> B) It has been manufactured under the supervision of an approved inspection authority, someone recognized by the chief inspector. (Our Chief Inspector being God).[19]

> C) The user is in possession of a certificate of manufacture, issued by the manufacturer ... tested in every respect. (The word of God says that he was tried and tested in every possible way, yet he never gave in to temptation).[20]

Jesus Christ is our "pressure vessel" for the "Digging a Well" Ministry.

> Spectacle Blinds – Keeping our perspective where it needs to be. We don't need to be swayed by the world and the things of the world that would pull us down.

---

[18] Hebrews 7:26
[19] Hebrews 12:18
[20] Hebrews 4:15

- Pipe Hanger Hardware – People that keep the weight evenly distributed so as not to put too much pressure on one person – (using our spiritual gifts to edify all of the body.)

- Spring Hangers – Keeping us from bottoming out or burning out.

- Constant Support – We all know that this ministry will need constant prayers and support of faithful men and women.

- Variable Support– Various kinds of support. Some people support by praying, or encouraging, and others by being servants or giving financially. We need others to just listen. Without each of them, we can't carry on our work.

Having all the equipment in place in order to be a pipeline to the lost world:[21]

THEN WE MUST WAIT ON THE LORD

A verse came to mind one morning while watering the yard. Seeing bird feathers everywhere, I picked them up. This caused me to look closer at the following verse.

But they that wait
upon the LORD

---
[21] LP Gas Calendar

DIGGING A WELL — GETTING READY FOR THE TRIP

> *shall renew their strength;*
> *they shall mount*
> *up with wings as eagles;*
> *they shall run,*
> *and not be weary;*
> *and they shall walk,*
> *and not faint.*
> *Isaiah 40:31*

Each time that I read this verse, I thought the Lord was telling me to sit still, listen and watch. Let's take a moment and dig deeper. Let's see if he might be saying something more than to just park and do nothing, just wait for him.

In Strong's Hebrew Concordance, the word "wait" is wak) havaq הוק-vaw'), which means, to bind together. We see the importance of binding together in

> *Two are better than one;*
> *because they have a good*
> *reward for their labour.*
> *For if they fall,*
> *the one will lift up his fellow:*
> *but woe to him that is*
> *alone when he falleth;*
> *for he hath not another*
> *to help him up.*
> *Again, if two lie together,*
> *then they have heat:*
> *but how can one be warm alone?*

> *And if one prevail against him,*
> *two shall withstand him;*
> *and a threefold cord*
> *is not quickly broken.*
> *Ecclesiastes 4:9-12*

First, we need to be entwined with the Lord. We need to be so interlocked with the Lord so that his ways become our ways.

Next, we need to have a close relationship with other Christians. These are people who can help us learn to study, pray, witness, and serve others better.

The more feathers a bird has, the more protection he has against the elements of nature. Surround yourself with other Christian brothers and sisters. Doing so will help protect you from the elements of the world.

You've heard the old saying, "Birds of a feather flock together."

Surrounding ourselves with other Christians gives us more stability and strength.

We have many birds in our trees. As I began to study the things that feathers do, I gained a new insight on Isaiah 40:31.

This is a list of the things that feathers are used for:
1. Protection from the weather
2. Controls body temperature
3. Swimming and diving
4. Floating
5. Balancing
6. Feeling
7. Hearing

8. Making sounds
9. Muffling sounds
10. Looking for food
11. Keeping Clean
12. Aiding digestion
13. Constructing nest
14. Transporting water
15. Escaping predators
16. Sending visual signals
17. Camouflage

When looking even further at the eagle I was even more amazed. The eagles have from 7,000 to 7,200 feathers on his wings. When the eagle is not in flight he preens his wings. His wings are made out of beta-keratin which is water resistant and wear resistant much like fingernails.

The eagle feathers have interlocking barbs and a special oily coating. When the eagle preens his wings the oil is secreted from a gland at the base of the tail or on the back. When the eagle is preening, what is taking place?

> Aligning together his feathers for optimum waterproofing and insulation.
> Aligning together his feathers into the most aerodynamic shape for easier, more efficient flight.
> Removing feather parasites and body lice that can destroy feathers or carry disease.
> Removing tough sheaths from newly molted feathers.

> Creating a healthier appearance to attract a mate.[22]

Now looking at the word, "wait" in this light, what do you think we should be doing?

Remember, the word "wait" means "to bind together" or renew our strength there are some things the Christian needs to do besides just sit and ponder what the Lord has in store for us.

Oil is mentioned repeatedly in the scripture as something we are to use. The eagle gains its strength from the oil and binding process. Shouldn't we take the example of the eagle and follow it?

Maybe the Lord is telling us something deeper than we have been seeing. We need to take the time and cleanse ourselves as the eagle does.

Wash me throughly from mine iniquity,
and cleanse me from my sin.
Psalm 51:2

The next step is to wait on the Lord. Take the time with your Christian brothers, to bind together, as the scripture says. While doing so, be sure and allow the oil of the Lord, the Holy Spirit, to empower you. Receive his anointing and you will be able to do as it says in Isaiah 40:31.

You will find the Lord has
renewed your strength;
and you shall mount up
with wings as eagles;

---

[22] http://askabiologist.asu.edu/content/23-functions-feathers
http://birding.about.com/od/birdbehavior/a/preening.ftm

DIGGING A WELL — GETTING READY FOR THE TRIP

you shall run,
and not be weary;
and you shall walk,
and not faint.

DIGGING A WELL
WHICH WELL WILL YOU DIG?

Lavished with new insights
When soaring to
New heights above

DIGGING A WELL — WHICH WELL WILL YOU DIG?

CONCLUSION

WHICH WELL WILL YOU DIG?

You may say, "I'm not digging a well." Oh, but my friend, you are. Every person that walks on the earth is digging some kind of a well. You may not want others to follow you but they will.

Some of us sit at the Well of Salvation. We are drinking from the salvation that the Lord has given us. As people pass by our well, we offer them safety. We tell them about Jesus Christ and how they can be saved and safe from an eternity in hell.

Some of us have drunk from the bitter water at Marah way too long. Now our children and grandchildren are drinking from that bitter water also.

People need to be introduced to Jesus Christ, the Living

| DIGGING A WELL | WHICH WELL WILL YOU DIG? |

Water. We need to pray for them daily. They may be broken and empty like the woman that came to Jesus at Jacob's well. Jesus knows their pain.

> *Brethren, I count not*
> *myself to have apprehended:*
> *but this one thing I do,*
> *forgetting those things*
> *which are behind,*
> *and reaching forth unto those*
> *things which are before,*
> *I press toward the mark for the prize*
> *of the high calling of God in Christ Jesus.*
> *Philippians 4:13-14*

The Lord may use you in the lives of others to
DIG A WELL

Embracing with awe and wonder
As the Spirit of God settles over your life,
Changing you into who you will become.

SETTING THE MARK

If I don't set a mark, no mark to recall

My dreams I'll accomplish, never walk, never fall

But if I set the mark right at my feet,

It doesn't take much, and then I'm in reach.

And if I set the mark closer, even closer to you,

I will have to stretch in order to view.

If I set the mark clear up to the sky,

Just trying a little will teach me to fly

If I set the mark as high as the stars,

I may not reach it but I'm a winner by far.

Where did you set it, the mark for your life?

Did you set it real low or did you set it real high?

The highest goal ever to be reached

Was set by Paul and thus we should teach.

It's the high calling of the Lord Jesus Christ

May we teach it and preach it until the day that we die.

Craving the purity of your presence,
Enduring, as the water crashes against my imperfections,
As the wall of nature starts falling down
And cleansing comes to my soul.

*JESUS, THE ROCK OF MY SALVATION,
THE WATER FOR MY SOUL,
PURIFYING THE DEEPEST PART OF ME
AS HIS SPIRIT, THROUGH ME, FLOWS.*

Made in the USA
Lexington, KY
11 November 2019